# THE FORBIDDEN

# THE
# FORBIDDEN

## POEMS FROM IRAN AND ITS EXILES

EDITED BY *Sholeh Wolpé*

MICHIGAN STATE UNIVERSITY PRESS ▪ *East Lansing*

⊖ The paper used in this publication meets the minimum requirements of ANSI/NISO Z39.48-1992 (R 1997) (Permanence of Paper).

 Michigan State University Press
East Lansing, Michigan 48823-5245

Printed and bound in the United States of America.

18  17  16  15  14  13  12     1  2  3  4  5  6  7  8  9  10

LIBRARY OF CONGRESS CATALOGING-IN-PUBLICATION DATA
The forbidden : poems from Iran and its exiles / edited by Sholeh Wolpé.
p. cm.
ISBN 978-1-61186-034-4 (pbk. : alk. paper) 1. Persian poetry—
Translations into English. 2. Exiles' writings, Persian—Translations into
English. I. Wolpé, Sholeh. II. Title: Poems from Iran and its exiles.
PK6449.E5F67 2012
891'.551308—dc23
2011024674

Cover design by David Drummond, Salamander Hill Design
(www.salamanderhill.com)

Book design by Charlie Sharp, Sharp Des!gns, Lansing, Mich.

Cover art is *Wall of Time* ©2010 and is used by permission of the artist,
Farbod Sadjadi.

green press INITIATIVE  Michigan State University Press is a member of the Green
Press Initiative and is committed to developing and
encouraging ecologically responsible publishing practices. For more
information about the Green Press Initiative and the use of recycled
paper in book publishing, please visit *www.greenpressinitiative.org*.

Visit Michigan State University Press on the World Wide Web at
*www.msupress.org*

*I Am Neda*

منم ندا

Leave the Basiji bullet in my heart,

fall to prayer in my blood,

and hush, father

—I am not dead.


More light than mass,

I flood through you,

breathe with your eyes,

stand in your shoes, on the rooftops,

in the streets, march with you

in the cities and villages of our country

shouting through you, with you.

I am Neda—thunder on your tongue.


—Sholeh Wolpé

بگذار گلوله آن بسیجی در قلبم بماند،

بر فرش خونم نماز بگذار.

خاموش، پدر!

من نمرده ام.


روحم همچو نور

در میان تو طغیان میکند؛

با چشمهایت نفس می کشم

کفش هایت را به پا می کنم

و در پشت بام ها می ایستم،

همراه تو پیش میروم

در خیابانها، در شهرها و روستاها؛

فریاد می زنم

با تو، از درون تو . . .

منم ندا—رعد بر زبانت


— شعله ولپی

# Contents

# Acknowledgments

First and foremost, I wish to thank the translators whose work appears in this anthology. Too often translators of poetry are not acknowledged or appreciated as they deserve to be. With that in mind, dear reader, I wish to bring these gifted individuals to your attention and note that without their talent and dedication we would not be able to enjoy the beauty and power of the poems in this anthology. I have provided the biographies of the translators at the end of the collection so you can get to know who they are.

I would like to extend wholehearted thanks to Dan Veach, publisher of the *Atlanta Review*, and to Martha Bates, acquisitions editor at the Michigan State University Press, for believing in the importance of this anthology and inspiring me to forge ahead to its completion. A debt of gratitude is also owed to the living poets in this collection who were generous with their work and time. A special thank you goes to my family for their unfailing support and encouragement.

This book is dedicated to the people of Iran and their struggle for peace, prosperity, and true democracy in that beautiful, ancient land.

# A Note to the Reader

When publisher Dan Veach asked me to edit the Iran issue of the *Atlanta Review*, neither of us dreamed it would become the journal's best-selling edition. Yes, Iran is a "hot topic" these days, but what seemed to impress those who read that issue were the poems themselves which represented poets living in Iran or in exile, political or not, dead or alive, ancient and modern.

Editor Martha Bates, from the Michigan State University Press, told me she could not put down the journal, that she read it from front to back, and would like to publish an expanded anthology. I was thrilled because now not only would I be able to include more poems by the same poets, but also include those I had painfully excluded from the *Atlanta Review* because of limited space.

Translation is important to me. As a poet I understand the sting of seeing one's poem mutilated in another language. As a literary translator I understand that a poetic translation is recreation, a re-rendering of what cannot be literally duplicated. As always, I have taken painstaking care that the new work translated for this anthology do justice to the poems themselves.

Make yourself a cup of tea, sit in a cozy chair, and enjoy this short anthology from cover to cover. You won't regret it.

# INTRODUCTION

One Saturday afternoon while walking down Melrose Avenue in Los Angeles, I gave into the urge to stop people at random and ask them what came to their minds when I mentioned Iran. Here are some of their responses: Islamic government, human rights violations, a nuclear threat, sponsors of terrorism, Holocaust deniers, women in veils, anti-Semites, Khomeini's fatwa on Salman Rushdie, enemies of Israel and the West, and the 1979 hostage crisis. Only one person had anything positive to say and it had something to do with a great kebab dish he had had at a Persian restaurant on Westwood Boulevard.

I was disheartened to find that few people had much regard for an ancient civilization rich in poetry and the arts—one credited with the invention of the windmill, refrigeration, the first teaching hospitals, alcohol in medicine, chess, polo, and even ice cream. Moreover, I suspect most Americans know very little about the role of the United States in Iran's recent history—the CIA backed coup that overthrew the democratic government of Mohammad Mosaddegh in 1953, the subsequent installation of Reza Shah, the support of the Shah's government despite his notorious human rights violations, and finally the sale of weapons to Saddam Hussein during the Iran-Iraq war. Why doesn't the average American know about these facts too? Perhaps the answer is that the citizens of any country, even those in a great democratic nation such as the United States, may often not be aware of their own governments' actions. A people is not always its government and conversely, a government does not always represent its people.

What *does* represent a people is their literature and the arts, ones created freely and not as a part of a propaganda machine. Poets, writers, and artists are able to gift us with the power of empathy. Their words, films, and canvases can serve as the antidote to the disease of apathy, and to the poison of religious and ideological fanaticism. I believe it is paramount that human beings throughout the world connect through the web of literature and culture. Otherwise we run the risk of perishing in the worst way possible—losing our humanity.

The brutal murder of Neda Agha-Soltan, a young Iranian woman who was killed on June 20, 2009, during a peaceful street demonstration in Tehran, brought the human struggle against a repressive regime closer to millions of people throughout the world. The Green Movement, formed after President Ahmadinejad's theft of the 2009 election, has become a struggle not only to conduct an honest and democratic electoral process but also to regain the most basic human rights so tragically lost after Khomeini's rise to power. The brutality of the present Islamic Republic, with its army of fanatical and well-funded Basiji militia, attacking the young and the old, women and children, is so shocking and widespread that even a number of their own clergy—such as the highly respected Ayatollah Montazeri (who passed away in December 2009)—have spoken loudly and vehemently against the present state of affairs. In Montazeri's words, the Islamic Republic of Iran has devolved into "a political system based on force, oppression, changing people's votes, killing, closure, arresting and using Stalinist and medieval torture, creating repression, censorship of newspapers, interruption of the means of mass communications, jailing the enlightened . . . and forcing them to make false confessions in jail."* He further declared the regime as "condemned and illegitimate."

Why did the people of Iran allow such a regime to take root in the first place? Two years before the 1979 revolution, The Writers' Association of Iran accepted an invitation from the Goethe Institute to organize its annual meeting. This resulted in an unprecedented ten nights of poetry readings heavy with political overtones. In a country where poets have the status of rock stars, these readings, which became known as *dah shab* (The Ten Nights), played a major contributing role in the Iranian revolution two years later. The diversity of views—leftists, Islamists, secular, etc.—were unified by a single resolve: to end the Shah's oppressive regime and bring about a prosperous democratic

---

*Los Angeles Times*, December 22, 2009.

government where freedom of expression, religion, and individual rights were respected and enforced.

The 1979 Iranian revolution was a people's revolution hijacked. Whether Muslim, Jewish, socialist, or atheist, all fought side-by-side to end one tyrannical regime to only find themselves in the clutches of another, even more ruthless and oppressive. Khomeini returned from exile and was supposed to act as a benevolent leader until a democratic government could be formed. Instead, appealing to the deep religious sensibilities of the masses, he promptly began to execute or banish anyone he considered a threat to the strict Islamic government he was planning to establish. The war with Iraq (1980–1988) only served to solidify his base by bringing the nation together to fight its common enemy. Voices were silenced, religious tolerance completely disappeared, women's rights were reduced to the theocrats' own interpretation of the Quran, non-Islamic music and literature was banned, dance was forbidden, and the freedom of press was squelched. In short, a dark world darkened even more and the torch bearers—the poets, writers, and artists—were driven deep underground.

But in a country like Iran, literature, particularly poetry, is like rain—it cannot be arrested. Vast umbrellas of censorship can be raised, people can be forced underground and into dungeons, but the water will eventually seep in, cleanse, nourish, and create a new landscape. This is true about many other countries and cultures. Indeed the first who recognize literature's power are the tyrants themselves. From Moscow to Beijing to Tehran, they fear the poets, jail them, torture them, and send them into exile, but they cannot silence their words.

As a strategy to combat the powerful voices of Iran's poets, the Islamic Republic began a campaign of advocating and creating their own brand of literature, enticing the younger generation, many of whom had been born under the repressive regime, with generous financial support to write, organize poetry workshops, and give readings. As a result a whole new brand of propaganda literature, produced in earnest, was born. This, they named Islamic literature. Yet, despite this clever effort, they could not suppress such untarnished voices as that of Simin Behbahani, whose poem "And Behold" is so well-known in Iran that it is often recited by heart. In this poem, Behbahani compares the camel's legendary rage with the anger brewing in people over a government controlling their destiny.

The poems I have selected for this anthology represent the young, the old, and the ancient. Although this anthology is divided into six sections, each a complete nugget, I suggest you read this collection from front to back because each poem is a musical note carefully sequenced so that by the time you finish the last poem you can hear the powerful symphony of the poets' voices.

I have included a good number of poems written in the diaspora. Historically, writing in exile has not been a part of the collective Iranian experience. However, what makes the Iranian exile poems interesting is that they are not homogeneous. One can observe a vast landscape of expressions and an arch of evolution in style and content that has richly developed over the course of the past thirty years. This is partly due to the extent of the dispersion of the poets throughout the world, a factor that has contributed to the color and dimension of the tapestry of Iranian poetry over all.

Despite the Islamic Republic's use of any and all available methods to quell dissent through all available means—including propaganda poems, novels, and films—in a country where even the uneducated bricklayers recite poems by heart, the voice of the poets cannot be silenced. Like rain it will seep into every crevice and feed the seedlings. In Iran's Green Revolution we see signs of saplings that have broken through pavements and are growing fast in the streets and squares. Anthologies such as this empower these saplings. This power does not just come from their fellow Iranians. Rather it comes from all human beings in every corner of the world; it comes from readers like you who allow in your lives the transformative power of literature.

# THE STATE OF RED

# And Behold

Simin Behbahani

*Do they not consider the camel, how it was created?*
—Qoran, Sura 88:17

And behold the camel, how it was created:
not from mud and water,
but, as if from patience and a mirage.
And you know how the mirage deceives the eyes.
And the mirage knows not the secret of your patience:
how you endure the thirst, the sand, and the salt marshes,
and gaze at the immense presence with your weary eyes.
And behold how this gaze is marked with salt grooves
like the dry lines remaining on your cheeks after a stream of tears.
And behold the tears that have drained from you
all means of consciousness.
With what nothingness should you fill this emptied space?
And behold in this emptied space the agitation of a thirsty camel,
made mad beyond the limits of its patience,
reluctant to carry meekly its heavy burden.
And behold its two incisors gleaming madly in a row of angry teeth.
Patience spawns hatred and hatred the fatal wound:
behold with what vengeance the camel
bit through the arteries of its driver.
The mirage lost its patience.
And behold the camel.

*Translated by* Farzaneh Milani *and* Kaveh Safa, *from*
A Cup of Sin, *courtesy of Syracuse University Press*

3

# In This Dead-End Road

AHMAD SHAMLOU

They sniff your breath
lest you have said: I love you.

They sniff your heart—
       (such strange times, my sweet)
and they flog love
at every checkpoint.

       We must hide love in the backroom.

In the cold of this dead-end crooked road
they stoke their pyres
with our poems and songs.

Don't risk thinking,
       for these are strange times, my sweet.

The man who beats at the door
in the nadir of night,
has come to kill the lamp.

       We must hide light in the backroom.

Those are butchers in passageways
with their chopping blocks
and bloodied cleavers.
       (such strange times, my sweet)
They hack off smiles from faces
and songs from mouths.

       We must hide pleasure in the backroom.

Canaries are barbequed
on flames of lilies and jasmines . . .
        (such strange times, my sweet)
and the devil, drunk on victory,
feasts at the table set for our wake.

        We must hide God in the back room.

        *Translated by* Sholeh Wolpé

# Death Sermon

NADER NADERPOUR

Hellish beast!
In my sight, you are a dark tempest
that has suddenly seized a thousand youthful leaves.
Let the wailing of your prisoners
grow so loud that they cannot be contained.
Let the flood of people's tears and blood flow
until the roses of revenge rise from the soil.

*Translated by* Sholeh Wolpé *and* Sahba Shayani

## The State of Red

MANDANA ZANDIAN

The stairway of our house was narrow
the stairway of our house was supposed to be
a place for hide-and-seek, for running up and down.
It was supposed to be white,
gleaming like the Milky Way.

The stairway of our house
was supposed to always laugh.

The air raid siren was red.
The siren cursed our stairway,
sullied it with darkness, dirt, and stench.
The siren smelled of hate.

The stairway of our house,
in its fear of the siren, collapsed
into itself and became a deep well,
dark, empty, and dry,
and inside it my dreams birthed headless nightmares
wrapped in layers of sounds—howls of jets and wolves.
My mother would press her head
against the stairway roof,
her pulse pounding in her eyes,
terrified lest she fall and be trampled
under our neighbor's pious feet—
the same neighbor who praised God incessantly
for the war's boundless bounties.

And my father would shoot my hands
with his eyes' bullets
all the way from the war at the border

so that he would not forget how young
I was, dying beside my dolls.

And Tehran . . .
never imagined it would become this red.
Its red sky and red earth
rumbled and quaked like thunder,
attacked our stairway with fury.

But tomorrow was always a new day!
A day where the earth became pregnant
with new parts of my classmates' dismembered arms.
A day of twenty new lies I could slurp up in our history class—
and our school believed it could look for shelter
during the geography lesson.
And God . . .
God always yawned.

*Translated by* Sholeh Wolpé

# Parts of a Pedestrian in a Tunnel

RASOUL YOUNAN

The sky was like an inverted beach
with blazing sand.
Punctured shoulders
kept alive the fear
that drilled itself into our bones.
Was it morning or evening?
We don't remember.
Were we awake or asleep?
We don't remember.
It was raining fire and sand,
still,
we don't remember anything.
We don't like
the police coming to our door.

We were four, all of us insane,
inside cubic nightmares,
and what we wished for
was for the sun to rise at midnight . . .
We pulled the bloodied sun
from the throats of roosters
and took to the streets.
In the streets they gave us plastic flowers
and we foolishly fell in love
and betrayed with sincerity.
This is how
our story became known to all.

We desired love
without its false trimmings,
a world without guns.
On dark walls

we painted red roses.
Passersby laughed at us.
Laughed at us, the passersby.
All we did
was look at them.
Roads
had knotted themselves around the city.
We stayed in the city, decaying and singing:
*The train that cannot carry us away from here
is not a train.*

We were big boys
with small desires.
We were the small desires of big boys.
And behind the doors and windows
the storm that dwelled, then subsided,
was the chronicle of our unfulfilled wishes.
We were four, all of us insane,
and our life
was a tragic pedestrian
in an obscure tunnel.
We were four, all of us insane.
Four teardrops
the world had shed . . .

We walked the streets until dawn.
Until dawn,
we walked the streets.
Yet both the street
and the night
were endless.

We danced in the moonlight—
        well, we were insane.
In the moonlight, we danced.
The city whirled around our heads.
Suddenly,
the police siren
halted our simple celebration.
We were afraid.
We shrank into a corner.
Later, the garbage collectors came.
They swept us away
along with all the dead leaves
and night's leftover garbage.
We were four pieces of rubbish—
they swept us away.
But the city remained full of trash.

*Translated by* Hassan Fayyad

# Of Sea Wayfarers

ESMAIL KHOI

> *Sign of a true lover is that he emerges cold from Hell*
> *Proof of a true wayfarer is that he comes forth dry*
> *from the sea.*
> —Sanaii

You alone have remained.

Those sea wayfarers
said:
from water we will come forth dry.
Riding on the waves of events, they said:
we hold the radium of vigilance
to whose lustrous, untouched core
particles of the dark have no passage.

Holding umbrellas of denial
                    they said:
we will survive the toxic rain,
they said:
even
            the storm's debris
            cannot devastate us.

They said . . .
They said . . .
They said . . . and

plain as day they saw
that behind the oysters' veil,
pearls
            —perhaps even blinded to themselves—
winked and consorted with corpses and grime,

as if they plainly understood
their vain umbrellas
were soon to become the swamp's wide lilies.

From afar, in the break of light,
they even watched the oysters
decay in the dark waters.
They saw;
and in a thousand mirrors, laughed.

You alone have remained.
Stay, alone.

*Translated by* Sholeh Wolpé

# Blood and Ash

NADER NADERPOUR

The earthquake that shook the house
recast everything in one night.
Like a flame, it burned the slumbering world,
filling its morning ash with blood,
hiding women's faces and flowers'
colors beneath rancor's soot.
It rocked death's cradle
and devoured people like a grave.
Beneath history's crumbling canopy
it galloped on the graves of kings.
It smashed ancient statues with no regard
for their makers' art.
It blocked the road of lovers' union,
shattered the lantern of the poets' inspiration,
tore out the instruments' melodious veins,
and drenched the chalice's brow with blood.
It buried deep in past sorrows
the priceless treasures of happy days.

*Translated by* Sholeh Wolpé *and* Sahba Shayani

# Camouflage Costumes

GRANAZ MOUSSAVI

The clamor of dusty children
changes in the throats of flutes.
For the children in narrow alleys, a gun
is two fingers put together;
and death
is closing of eyelids and rolling around in dirt.
Tomorrow
imaginary guns shall be left and forgotten
on the decks of paper boats,
and the camouflage costumes, once too large for the world's children
shall fit.

*Translated by* Sholeh Wolpé

# Untitled

SHAMS LANGEROODI

1.

Look how they have watered the trees
so that instead of fruit they bear pigeon eggs;
how they have swept the streets
so that it is empty of people;
how they have told me
that if I write four more poems
you would come—but now say
that I must return and rendezvous with you
at the start my poems.

But I will not erase these verses,
for one day or night you will come.
It is even possible you may crack out of an egg
of a Simourgh-like bird, a bird
who in Attar's Conference of the Birds
began as *Si Mourgh*—thirty birds—
to finally become one: The One.
But we—
we were one who became many.

2.

I miss you;
until I'm happy again
tree branches shall grow in your shape;
a small bird whose name I do not know
shall pour your name on my book;
the sun, shape of a copper butterfly,
shall flutter about my voice.
I know that silence is silent because of me
but I miss you and I push away
my words so I can see you.

3.

Many poets
grow old without a song or a poem,
searching for their other halves.

Many poets
leaf through pages of darkness to the end,
searching for a patch of light.

Many poets
who have no pens, pen poems
with the fingertips of the wind,
iridescent as bubbles upon water.

How leaf and pen are wasted in forests
that shade birds—wordless, pen-less birds
who orate with songs while
half lit by light, half hidden in shade.

*Translated by* Sholeh Wolpé *and* Ahmad Karimi-Hakkak

# *A MOB! TUMULT!*

PEYMAN VAHABZADEH

Six billion people
　　　　　—shift and shove—
　　　　　　　　　　waiting in line

(You see, tonight
　　　　they are supposed to shoot all poets.)

I look everywhere
but can't find myself.
I am terrified.

"Don't be afraid! Maintain a revolution-style calm!
Those of you whose turn has not come tonight feel
assured that we will hang you by next week!"

I am relieved.
I'm sure I'll find myself
　　　　　　　　by then.

*Translated by* Sholeh Wolpé

# My House Is Cloudy

Nima Yushij

My house is cloudy.
The whole earth is cloudy too.

The wind—desolate, broken, and drunk—
roars through the pass,
lays waste to the world,
and to my senses too.

Piper, you whom your melody's charm
has steered you far from this road,
where are you?

My house is cloudy,
and the clouds are on the verge of rain.
I dream of the bright days I let drift away and vanish.
I face the sun, the open sea,
but the world now lays in ruins from the wind,
and the piper, ever-playing his song,
makes his own path in this cloud-afflicted world.

*Translated by* Sholeh Wolpé

# Blood's Voice

MOHSEN EMADI

If one day flood brings in a sad panther
and a shrine's door,
if they sew up a shirt with the panther's skin,
make a necklace with his teeth,
I know that whoever puts on the shirt
will disappear,
and whoever wears the necklace
would be obliged to carry
her own head under her arms.

I take the shrine's door
install it on the threshold
of my house. It creaks open
to a circle of women,
heads on knees,
caressing their own hair.

Outside, body-less heads
surround a fire with songs.
I don't recognize my own voice
and the door closes and opens
to the rhythm of the words I grunt.

It is raining.
An unclothed woman knocks on the door.
She carries a boat on her back.
I greet her between the panther's roar
and the door's groans.
Silently she unloads her boat in a corner,
climbs in and falls asleep.

The house is in water.
Water carries away corpses of women,
it carries away the door,
and my voice.

We paddle.
We row looking for the voice.

My legacy is a door through which
when a woman enters or leaves
my voice cracks,
and the house drowns in that alien sound.

Each time my bed is a boat
to attract the nudity of a woman.
A woman's nakedness is silent.
It is wet.

I uproot the door,
plant it on my rooftop.
The wind blows.
Guns appear on the threshold of the door.
They point themselves at my throat.

The wind blows
and a thousand wounded panthers
leap out from my mouth.
I am naked.

An unclothed woman,
wet,
draws herself out from among the guns,

kisses the door,
kneels before me.
Panthers leap out from her hair.

I caress your hair.
The door will shut,
voices and winds will pound on the door.
I will not open.
And the lost voice of the man
will become blood,
will flood through the cracks
and mingling with the rain
that will come pouring,
it will flow through the city's gutters and veins.
I kiss you
and my blood leaps out with every breath,
out from my throat.
It becomes my voice.

You are silent.
You speak inside me.

There's no one on the rooftop.
I stand there, collect all the photographs
the shirts, the photos of a thousand hands holding guns,
the portraits of women's heads
and the narrow stream of blood
that flows on the paper's edge.

I light a match,
throw into fire the shirts and the papers.
The fire has your shape.

I want to touch your hair.
I reach for you
and become a poet.

I pick up my pen
and blood flows from my hand.
The lines are your hair,
in every line a panther roars.

On the balcony
I fill my childhood cradle with soil,
plant roses inside it.
I water the roses.
I rock the cradle.
The city is silent.

*Translated by* Sholeh Wolpé

# If Rising from Your Grave

NAANAAM

If rising from your grave you water
the flowers on your tombstone
before returning to the earth again
tomorrow everyone will accuse you of dying.
Better to remain dead.
Are you afraid of death? Death means
life without the "I'm afraid of death."

If rising from your grave you recite
a prayer by your tombstone
everyone will say you're dead.
Better to remain dead.

*Translated by* Peyman Vahabzadeh *and* Roger Humes

# Death from the Window

Naanaam

Death from the window happens twice:
once when it's rainy and
once when it's rainy
again.

*Translated by* Peyman Vahabzadeh *and* Roger Humes

# *Life*

NAANAAM

Life is a glove
and the hand,
death.

*Translated by* Peyman Vahabzadeh

# The Sticky Dream of a
# Banished Butterfly (Excerpt)

MARYAM HOOLEH

The flower I sent you yesterday       wilted on the way
THIS IS THE MEANING OF BANISHMENT, I know!
But smell its stem!

        *I'm still coming towards you. . . .*


Civilization     has devoured my fears
     I no longer fear beheadings     on my breathing platter!
It would have been fair if at least
     I would have had a hand in MY OWN DIGNITY
Is smiling     mandatory?     To increase my card's privileges
with my uniform and hair dye!?
*Me whose lines are unclear*     in this revolt for selfhood
     in a bourgeois scheme I have no color in!

27

     In a free European country
     A naked gene     tans under the sun, like everyone else
     It's hard to know how far *humanity here* will take us!
     I don't fear the sting of mosquitoes
     But if I leave my body     whose uniform will I be?
     I take issue with my soul     since it became a socialist
on Resurrection day
Paranoia . . . paranoia . . .
*Halleluja . . . Halleluja . . .*


I want my hands
My glasses     The dead borders of happiness!
GIVE ME BACK MY COLORS!
I want my differences
     My bad luck, my birth certificate

I want the earth          to drop dead!
*Headless, Civil Society is posing*
          *in its uniform for a black and white photograph!*

*Translated by* Niloufar Talebi

# Our Tears Are Sweet

Simin Behbahani


Our tears are sweet, our laughter venomous.
We're pleased when sad, and sad when pleased.
We wash one hand in blood, the other we wash the blood off.
We cry as we laugh at the futility of both these acts.
Eight years have passed, we haven't discovered their meaning.
We have been like children, beyond any account or accounting.
We have broken every stalk, like a wild wind in the garden.
We have picked clean the vine's candelabra.
And if we found a tree, still standing, defiantly,
we cut its branches, we pulled it by the roots.
We wished for a war, it brought us misery,
now, repentant, we wish for peace.
We pulled wings and heads from bodies,
now, seeking a cure, we are busy grafting.

Will it come to life, will it fly,
the head we attach, the wing we stitch?


*Translated by* Farzaneh Milani *and* Kaveh Safa

# I See the Sea . . .

SHAMS LANGEROODI

I see the sea shrink
then shrink again
until it fits in the palm of my hand.

And I
hear the sound of flying fish,
the dead sailors' cough, the burning whales,
the shivering mermaids, the horses and the wind,
the sea's white curls,
and the drowned strangers who have forgotten their human voice.

I see
the sea
      shrink
      then shrink even more
the oars' hopeless beats,
the foam-circled boats,
the frozen shadows,
the salt encrusted stores,
the disheveled hopeless left on the shore . . .
Oh what strange mystery,
the sea!

I see your purple fingers
in the beakers of the dead,
and the shoulders of the wind
drenched with your mouth's sweat,
and I see your bitter joy.

I see
the sea
shrink,

then shrink again,
and I
float farther
from the invisible shore.

Where is this familiar boat
whose oars' solemn sound mingles
with the rain carrying us?

*Translated by* Sholeh Wolpé

# You Said, It's Only Grapes

SIMIN BEHBAHANI

You said, it's only grapes. I said, I don't see any!
You said, believe me. I will pick you some.
This is the garden of history and these the vines
that bear fruit each year in great abundance and variety.
You gestured with your hands as if you were picking grapes.
You said, close your eyes and open your mouth,
I will let you taste one that is firm and sweet.
I did as you told me. Ugh! How salty it was!
It tasted of vomit and blood. I spat it out.
It was an extracted eyeball.
It was as if the ceiling had collapsed on my head.
It was as if the world had started rolling like a millstone.
It was as if the stars and the moon were raining blood.
You said, it's only grapes. I screamed,
I see nothing on the vines but eyeballs.

*Translated by* Farzaneh Milani *and* Kaveh Safa

# TRANSLATING SILENCE

# *Me*

GRANAZ MOUSSAVI

I'm neither a person, nor a finch
I'm just a small accident
that happens every time
and I break in two
one half swept off by the wind
the other, by a man I do not know.

*Translated by* Sholeh Wolpé

# *The Poem*

MOHSEN EMADI

*For Reza A'lameh-zadeh*

1.

Words are the burying ground of things.
The trot of a horse through these lines
is a sound I haven't heard since childhood.
Your laughter wilted in my teenage years.
I write
as if on pilgrimage to the city of the dead.
If time by chance slips backwards,
my father's murmurs will echo
in the ears of the text, the sound of a bullet
will disturb the sleep of these lines
and a wild-haired poem will pace
a room that's been decayed for years.
Words have been arranged along the faded lines of a house:
Here is a window,
behind the window a courtyard. No one knows
which nightmare awakens the poem. It sees
sometimes, at the window, the glance of a neighbor's bride,
sometimes the swing and the bicycle,
or the wall with its cheap paintings.
It looks at them
until they come alive
then, to the inhale and exhale of living things
goes back to sleep.

2.

Years ago my father's murmurs
lost their way in the text of sleep
and the poem lit three thousand candles,

built three thousand paper boats
and offered them all to the sea.
Now that I have packed my bags
and wait for the first train
that would not return me here,
the poem is riding a bicycle;
trembling and in haste
it pedals through bumps and puddles,
rings a door bell, stares at whispers and sobs
afraid of being heard.
But the whispers are so loud in the ear
it is impossible to hear the whistle of a train.
I am still in the station
and the poem in *Khavaran**
protects the dead of these past years
from the gaze of the guards.

3.
A year ago
the poem slipped through barbed wire
where soldiers patrolled the hills of your breasts,
stole your lips,
your hands;
recreated you piece by piece.
This year, soldiers guard the edge of nothing:
your body long stolen.
In the station,
my bench is occupied by a dead
whose name the poem doesn't know.

---

*Located in the southeast of Tehran, *Khavaran* was a Baha'i cemetery later used for prisoners of conscience killed in the mass execution of 1988. It was reportedly demolished by the government in January 2009.

(It wouldn't learn your name either.)
Bullets and warm blood
find their way into the lines—
no paper can stop the bleeding.
The station is full of passengers who are dead.
The firing squads,
and the hanging ropes
are not waiting for any train.
Mumbling grave-diggers
ring the doorbells of three thousand homes.
Three thousand abandoned bicycles
litter the alleys.


    4.

The poem is not standing in front of a firing squad.
Nor does the firing squad
know where, on the poem, to aim at.
They simply hike the price of utilities,
the rent, and burial expenses.
I cannot buy cigarettes for three thousand dead
but I can bring them all back to life.
I don't want to make the poem
send them back to a cemetery
that doesn't exist anymore;
I only want to remind it
that all the abandoned bicycles have decayed by now,
that no one will ever again hear the jangle of their bells.
The dead will remain in the station
and if the poem can secure a ticket from each reader
it will send them off on the first one-way train.
In my country

three thousand dead in a station is normal.
Three thousand dead on a train is normal.

5.
At the border stations
they arrest our tongues.
Our words decay when they cross that line.
I let go of your hands outside the station,
the train's whistle hurries my words.
Words have filled up all the cabins,
they dream thousand-year nightmares.
My words are young,
just thirty years old,
but they have piled up
layer by layer
under this prison garb.
Yellow was not the color of my first school shoes,
nor was red the color of my piggy-bank,
or blue the color of my first bicycle.
Words grew up with the colors of your dress;
they were a herd of fleeing horses,
a rainbow that you would take off
and send curving through the air,
falling into mud and dirt,
into handcuffs, darkness, and the command to shoot.

6.
I'm not standing in this long line for bread and milk.
I stand here to surrender my tongue.
Everything crossing the border becomes lighter.
I stand to be translated.

A bicycle rides my borders
over bumps and puddles.
The poem considers conjunctions and prepositions,
the distance between I and I,
the me to-from-on-or me.
It is raining
on conjunctions and prepositions,
on relationships.
In the rain
the distance between us widens,
and in that distance, *Khavaran* grows larger.

7.

In my language
every time we suddenly fall silent
a policeman is born.
In my language
on the back of each frightened bicycle
sit three thousand dead words.
In my language
people murmur confessions,
dress in black whispers,
are buried
in silence.
My language is silence.
Who will translate my silence?
How am I to cross this border?

*Translated by* Shirindokht Nourmanesh,
Dan Veach, *and* Sholeh Wolpé

# From "23"

The airplane
has landed.
White smoke-loaded smile:
what a cargo
of sorrow.

A silent rain
surrounds the airport.
A tattered wet wind
chases black pigeons.
White smoke-loaded smile:
what a cargo
of sorrow.

Bodies came back on ice.
Corroded hopes
falling off piece by piece.

Handless shadows,
directionless clocks.
Fathers
who against the storm
bow their heads to inner ground
turn to ashes.
Mothers
who know not
to what punishment they were born.

The airplane
has landed.
Wounded soldiers

take shelter in each other's arms,
frostbitten birds in the sleet.

White smoke-loaded smile:
what a cargo
of sorrow.

Look
a bird has split in two.
The sky is torn in shreds, and song and light
        gush from its heart.
Rain and wind, a phrase of taps, a branch of bitter orange
        gush from its heart.

Come
let's gather the fragments of birds
        and make a little song,
        and hide in its delicate shelter.
There's nothing
        to hang on to
                in this fiery whirling wind.

Look!
A thimble
has made room for two pale lakes
to drown me.
A drought year
is hiding in the plumbing
to swallow me.
The mud-colored wardrobe
is a crucifix on the hilltop
of my scattered clothes.

There's nothing
　　　to hang on to
　　　　　in this fiery whirling wind.

The airplane
has landed.
A headless commander
shouts orders
at burnt corpses.

Dogs bark
among metallic stars
and red and yellow
a skull
on command
stands at attention.

*Translated by* Zara Houshmand

# The Shah and Hosseinzadeh

Reza Baraheni

the Shah has granted full authority
to Hosseinzadeh

once he mustered six of us        blindfolded
we were loaded on a truck        an hour before
dawn they took us out of the city        then they
brought us back to the city        it was
as though we were traveling from one city
to another in our dreams        then we were
unloaded and bound to six iron posts
then the command of that familiar voice was heard:
squad!
attention!
prepare to fire!
fire!

all six of us pissed our pants!

they removed our blindfolds
Hosseinzadeh and Azudi stood in a corner
pissing themselves with laughter!

say *Doctor* Hosseinzadeh! and *Doctor* Azudi!

*Translated by* Michael Henderson *and* Reza Baraheni

44

# Hosseinzadeh, the Head Executioner

REZA BARAHENI

Azudi lights his cigarette
—say *Docto*r Azudi!
       and *Doctor* Hosseinzadeh!—
he's short, with a bald head, and eyes uneasy
as the asshole of a nervous rooster
he is a man of great renown:
he always stubs his cigarette on the back of a human hand
he never smokes more than forty a day
and the first caress is always
the privilege of this *Pahlavi* slut
and the last caress too
between the two cuffs
Azudi and Rassuli and Shadi and Manuchehri
Azudi and Parvizkhan and Rezanvan and Hesseini nurse
       the patient
one extracts his nails
another his teeth
a third scours the skin
a fourth provides the shock treatment
a fifth the re-flagellation
and the sixth prepares the ailing for the *coup de grace*
there's a short man whose name is Ardalan
       —say *Doctor* Ardalan!—
he fucks the afflicted
man and woman are the same to him
he holds a Ph.D. in rapacity

(and you, prisoner! you try all this time to forget
the name of the half-blind man who printed that
article of yours. He has a wife, three children, a
father, and a mother, and he provides for them all)

and then Hosseinzadeh
      —say *Doctor* Hosseinzadeh!—
administers the final cuff
the final verdict to shoot you
comes between the two caresses

*Translated by* Michael Henderson *and* Reza Baraheni

# Ass Poem

Reza Baraheni

When a thick-necked agent rides your neck
and your pants are pulled down to your knees
When two rape-kings politely offer each other your ass
        saying, "You first"
One
is not reminded of long ants with
one leg broken and the other leg
unable to carry the ant
And one is not reminded of the words of his late grandmother to
learn perseverance from the ants who
run fearlessly on and on—
even if they may have lost their heads and asses—
One is not reminded of Mozaffaruddin Shah who died of a hernia
or Reza Shah who died of syphilis
One is not reminded of the blond girl
whose womb the Shah recently inflated
One is not reminded of his consumptive Aunt
One is not reminded of anything at all
Only
he sees a beast bigger than himself
piercing through the depths of his bones
and the spell of degradation is nailed into his bloody ass hole
as if the order "Wanted: Dead or Alive"
was tacked on his ass
And then one addresses his mother in his mind
saying
Why
don't you pull me up the way you put me down, why?

*Translated by* David St. John *and* Reza Baraheni

# *Depression*

YADOLLAH ROYAI

One heart was beating between us,
one heart was beaten between us
when suddenly
we were led out of that small familiar cell.
Prison walls lined up
to prevent passage to the other side.
Each time a passerby coughed
on the other side of the window,
a star released a dagger.

This side of the window,
once every 24 hours
a whip reared its head from the calendar.
The rock's large heart did not beat
and the leaf could not hear
its own heartbeat
except in the rain.

Calendar, whips
and wide walls
escorted us past
24 coughs,
24 daggers.

*Translated by* Sholeh Wolpé *and* Ahmad Karimi-Hakkak

# Petition

Nader Naderpour

I was reading about and witnessing
how this land of world-conquering kings
has become history's eternal ruin.
As twisted fate would have it,
I was born in this ruinous land,
a land that's not a sanctuary of compassion
but the prison of the heralds of the sun;
the realm of the protectors of darkness
hostile to revolutionaries.
What language is more reviled here
than the one I use?
From time immemorial the recipient
of its words have been their own speakers.
Meaning: my mouth and two lips
mask every word in fear of thought censors.

*Translated by* Sholeh Wolpé *and* Sahba Shayani

# A List of Names

PARTOW NOORIALA

*In Evin prison in Tehran, each evening they announce the names*
*of those to be executed later in the night. Prisoners keep their hopes*
*alive by planting the seeds of their sorghum brooms in their cells.*

A list of names
is waiting
for the night's turn.
I have come
as far as the light's last ray.
The bashful sun, ashamed,
melts away
at the bitterness of my glare.

The names are announced.
My chest splits open.

A storm of sounds
carries your bright name
to its vortex.
The rain that pounds on the doors,
the earth, whose cracks are healing,
and an invisible lily
that grows from my chest
are the absolute presence
of your name.

Time blazes.
I am tossed to the far side
of the world.
Years, stone-hard and quicksilver,
tear open memories,
but still

I use the spell of your name
to get through dreams,
through closed eyelids,
to spend my ration of hope.

With your name
I pass through walls,
through locked doors,
through the sound of the typewriter,
the copy machine and the computer,
through foreign languages,
through newspapers,
through the news.
I pass through picture frames
and in a pool of brilliant water
I see your image
in the shape of
a Nicaraguan man,
a Chilean woman,
a Jewish-Arab child.

Roads merge,
languages are blood kin,
and wide-split chests
are landscapes of astounding resemblance.

The sun
begins to shine again.
A woman, pierced with lilies,
passes through the walls
in search of you.

The seeds of the broom
that you planted
in your moldy prison
have made a green meadow
on the salt flat.

*Translated by* Zara Houshmand

# Nargess

Partow Nooriala

Hey, Nargess, Primrose, Nargess,
winter has wafted in your scent,
voices have brought your name.

If you, with your guileless eyes,
believed an ideology that was all fire,
then, why worry?
You sprouted out pure
from your flowerbed.

Hey, love-drunk Nargess!
Angel in human form!
When your loins
trembled with labor pain,
and they wanted your eyes
to see only the dark,
when on that abandoned island
poisonous weeds shrouded your body,
your pain sprouted out of you
in a human form,
and the scent of primrose
painted the Tehran sky lemon gold.

*Translated by* Sholeh Wolpé

Nargess, a young Iranian woman, was arrested because of her political activism against the Islamic
Republic of Iran. Blindfolded, she gave birth to her first child, in Tehran's notorious Evin prison.
Nargess in Persian means Primrose, a fragrant flower.

# *Always the Same . . .*

AHMAD SHAMLOU

Always the same . . .

Sorrow
the same:
an arrow stuck in your side, to the hilt,
consolation
the same:
compose an elegy.

Sorrow the same, signs of sadness the same
object of the elegy
different.

Always the same
the ruse
            the same . . .
night the same and darkness the same
so that the lamp
can forever remain an emblem of hope.

The path the same
and exhaustion
            the same,
so when you encounter the word "horseman"
your audience should think a savior is on the way.

And thus it was—and is
that the dictionary
was entrusted to the interrogators
so they can enchain every word
                        that bears a load of meaning.

And leave the words with no sense

to poets.


And words were cast into four groups:
free-spirited and senseless
political and senseless
emblematic and senseless
insulting and senseless.


And out of the most senseless words
poets carved so many signifiers of sin
that the interrogators, now out of patience,
changed their way.


And thereafter
speaking itself was the crime!

*Translated by* Ahmad Karimi-Hakkak

# I Did Not Expect

AHMAD REZA AHMADI


I did not expect to come face to face
with this absolute snow.

I did not expect to come face to face
with this absolute love.

These sleeping birds on the glazed tiles
portend this pure love will melt
in that pure snow.

If only you knew
how I set fire to the vine.
On that Friday I understood
there wasn't even time
to deny that absolute love.

I have seen through a lifetime
so many scarred ashtrays belonging to men now dead,
been witness to so many desolate days
that I need no one to tell me how things stand.

At times I witnessed the life of a matchstick flame
outlast my friends' lives.
At times I watched someone in search of an address in the rain,
someone whom as soon as I showed the way,
suddenly burst into flames and turned to ashes.
How I have consoled everyone
that this street shall end,
and how they have consoled me
that at the end of this street
a basket of grapes waits for me.

I entrust this absolute love
to the pages of the Divan of Hafiz.
Until when?
I do not know.
Until what hour?
I cannot tell.

*Translated by* Sholeh Wolpé *and* Ahmad Karimi-Hakkak

# Of Your Uncles

AHMAD SHAMLOU

*For little Siavash*

Not for the sake of the sun
but for the sake of a tiny rooftop shadow,
not for the sake of epics
but for the sake of a song
      smaller than your hands.

Not for the sake of forests
or for the sea
but for a leaf,
for a drop
      brighter than your eyes.

Not for the sake of walls
but for the sake of a fence,
not for the sake of the world
but for the sake of your home
and for your childish certainty
that each person is a world.
For the sake of my wish to be with you
even for a moment,
for your small hands in my big hands,
and my large lips
on you innocent cheeks.

For the sake of a dove inside a breeze
      when you shriek with excitement,
for the sake of dew on a leaf
      when you sleep,
for the sake of a smile
      when you see me beside you.

For the sake of a ballad,
a story on the coldest night, on the darkest night,
for your dolls, not for the sake of big people,
for a cobble stone path that leads me to you,
not for the sake of distant highways.

For the sake of a drainpipe when it rains,
for the sake of hives and honey bees,
for a cloud's white proclamation in the big serene sky.
For your sake,
for the sake of everything small
and everything pure
they fell to the ground.
Remember them.
I speak of your uncles.
I speak of Morteza.*

*Translated by* Sholeh Wolpé

---

*Morteza Keyvan (1922–1954) was an Iranian poet, writer, and journalist who was executed by the Shah's government a year after the U.S. led coup in Iran against the democratically elected government of Mohammad Mosaddegh.

# 99 NAMES OF EXILE

# 99 Names of Exile

KAVEH BASSIRI

| | | |
|---|---|---|
| Adam & Eve | Fugitive | Stranger |
| Afflicted | Guilty | Street Arab |
| Afraid | Heretic | Terrorist |
| Alien | Homeless | Traitor |
| Banished | Homesick | Trespasser |
| Beggar | Impure | Unclean |
| Castaway | Infectious | Uncorrectable |
| Colonist | Inhuman | Undesirable |
| Condemned | Insurgent | Undomesticated |
| Crippled | Invisible | Unfit |
| Dangerous | Ishmael | Unfortunate |
| Dark | Jew | Unidentified |
| Deportee | Kashmiri | Uninvited |
| Deserter | Lost | Unknown |
| Detested | Malefactor | Unnamed |
| Different | Marooned | Unrecognized |
| Dirty | Mysterious | Unskilled |
| Disgraced | Nigger | Unspeakable |
| Disinherited | Non-citizen | Unthinkable |
| Dismissed | Non-conformist | Untouchable |
| Disowned | Other | Unusual |
| Displaced | Outcast | Unwanted |
| Dispossessed | Outlaw | Unwilling |
| Dyke | Outsider | Unworthy |
| Emigrant | Overseas | Victim |
| Ethnic | Pariah | Villain |
| Evil | Queer | Virus |
| Exotic | Refugee | Wanderer |
| Expatriate | Resident Alien | Witch |
| Expelled | Runaway | Wrong |
| Extraterrestrial | Scapegoat | X |
| Foreign | Squatter | Yellow |
| Forsaken | Stateless | Zero |

63

# Ghazal 2

NADER NADERPOUR

Ancient motherland.
Land of my beloved.
I tore my heart away from you,
but if I flee to where must I flee,
and if I stay, where can I stay?
I have neither the legs for leaving,
nor the strength to remain.
I am like a barren tree
and it would not be strange if
the axe-wielding cutter covets my bones.
How can a celestial flower bloom and release
its perfume in this hell?
Spring! What will I gain from your
rain when I am the essence of fall.

*Translated by* Sholeh Wolpé *and* Sahba Shayani

# Spring Story

NADER NADERPOUR

I said to myself,
man dispossessed of your country,
why have you turned away from the world?
Live in this city of your asylum
as if this is your land.
Leave your house each night
to savor a glass of red wine.
In every lane and alley,
myriad beauties come and go.
Take one of them as lover and imagine
that beneath the pale blue sky
there is no one but you and her.

My heart heard all this and
rejuvenated, abandoned despair.
I taught my lips to smile,
pulled on my clothes and left
the house with such joy
that my sorrow withdrew in shame.

I had taken no more than two steps
when an old beggar blocked my way.
He was clad in rags and held tight
an empty wine bottle in his hands.
The spring clouds suddenly began to weep
drenching the soil with God's taintless tears.
I saw my own reflection in his eyes:
a man like him, dressed in rags.
I looked all around, there was no one else,
just us, two homeless wanderers
one sober, the other drunk.

When light broke through the clouds
the old man vanished as well.

I said to myself,
man dispossessed of your country,
even your shadow deserts you.
Do not leave this eternal exile,
for your future is no better than today!
What hope can one not blessed in the past,
harbor for the future?
The twilight was half alive when night arrived.
The world wept bitterly inside its smile.

*Translated by* Sholeh Wolpé *and* Sahba Shayani

# Marco Polo

ALI ALIZADEH

Maybe it's the natural
extension of immigration. Maybe

it's the awesome travel
bugs, making my wife's feet

uncommonly itchy. I'm not
surprised, at any rate, to hear

the pediatrician's nickname
for our son. 'Marco Polo' suits

his—in utero—trajectory
along the Silk Road, from

Kublai Khan's Forbidden City
to the snow-covered stones of a caravanserai

in central Turkey. Not to mention
the Australian interregnum

where ultrasound scans
revealed his sex. But our Marco

probably won't pen a Travels
as he won't know the other side

of unending expedition, say
cherished waterways of Venice, in short

a concrete home. Are we monstrous
parents? Why have we conceived

and delivered a life unto the world
in transition? If held to account

by a solicitous young man
with my eyes (and my wife's better

eyebrows) one day, accused
of depriving him of his deserved

comforts of sedentary genesis
(motherland, mother tongue

two ebullient grandmothers, etc.)
I can only offer an image: removing

picture frames, tribal ornaments
from the hooks; clearing the drawers

of wrinkled notepads with withered ideas
and perforated socks; tearing

the hooks off the walls. And then
the bright outline of the picture frames

vacated on the otherwise drab
dust-darkened surface of the wall. It's this

record of the passage of time
the contrast between the original

shade and color
and the rest (ditto our lives) dog-eared

by mould, sunlight, scratches
of nature and accidents. It's this

visible discrepancy between
what we were and what we've become,

the chance to uncover
and see it. The nomads treasure,

wisdom: the reality of aging
towards death. You see, Marco

—I'll tell him—if we can see
death looming, like a dark island

on the navigator's horizon
then we won't be shocked when

time's run out. This means
a life without our primal fear. That's why

we travel.

# Red-Raft Woman

ESTHER KAMKAR

In another country
at the edge of the river
I talk to the red-raft woman:
Ask me and I'll tell you
about my sister.

How we grew old without
each other's stories,
how our children never
slept like seals side by side
on Grandma's living room floor;
her children never asked me
for midnight pancakes.

Red-raft woman
make me a map
and I'll show you
where I was years ago —
Buffalo, Niagara Falls.
No one ever told me
about the sound —
how it vibrates and embraces you.

The joy of holding my sister
after twenty eight years,
the silence after the Falls.
What roared in me was
the grief-sound of absence.

O, and her granddaughters,
the mountain slope and wild poppies
behind her house, and her garden
blooming with tea rose from Kashan.

# Map of Ashen Roads

SHOLEH WOLPÉ


To put a cigarette between her fingers, just so,
bring it to her lips and inhale, just so,
launch smoke rings in the air, just so.
What could be *cooler* than that?

This is how she dips her finger
in cigarette ash and draws
clouds beneath her toes
a bridge of hearts to a six bedroom house,
a tall spectacled spouse, a German Shepherd,
awards, diplomas, pictures
of love under sheets soft as moss
and green as the sea inside her womb,
of rainy Sunday mornings with pancakes,
her children barely out of dreams, sweet
hot butter dripping from their mouths,
New Year pajama parties with friends,
a secret herb garden behind a rusty door.

Beneath this blizzard of ashes
a husband examines her head
with a stethoscope, declares her absurd,
her son lives and dies, dies and lives again,
her tongue sprouts swollen wings,
a gun smokes against a beloved forehead,
and the willow in the yard weeps its sap.

In Tehran the bird's egg hatches a cat,
her childhood house coughs black smoke
and roads turn to dead-end alleys.

Over it all she draws a lover, pours
her dark curls like tar into his hands,

feeds words to a locomotive train
bound for a place called *away*,
and tells herself, this is exile.

And in the end, her face a map of ashen roads,
she goes to the sink, lathers and rubs,
slowly raises her chin to the mirror.
And stares.

# Memorial Day

Kaveh Bassiri


Everyone loves me. At the gate, they rush to greet me, want to know
what I bring, make sure I packed correctly, examine me to see how I'm
doing.

My name is as unique as an article, as useful as the shah of shahs, Light
of Aryans.

My language, an Arabesque English dining room, where children
wrestle in Persian, fight over America and abgusht.

The flag of my country isn't a white towel. It's hairy and brown with a
big nose.

I'm Pythagorean. I believe in numbers, the orchestra of tangents and
cosines. I attend to cell phones, emails; memorize licenses, alarm
codes, credit cards, passports, passwords.

My family loves divorces. My father divorced twice. I divorced my
country twice.

The dark in the caves of my eyes is so precious they've designed
software to detect it.

My soul is a wreck; everyone slows down to watch what happened.

My questions are like electrons; they know where I am, but they don't
know where to take me.

They're auctioning my happiness on the shores of eBay.

My enemies care a great deal, know me well. My friends ask them
about me.

Somewhere in the east, my sentence is being finished for me.

My absence is momentous. When I left Tehran, a revolution swelled in my place. When I left Berlin, the wall came down. And when I leave tomorrow, the airports will close.

Each morning, in order not to sink, I have to bail the news out of me.

My faith is a soiled soap lathering the fields of continents.

I do ablution with Old Spice.

My failures are enormous; they keep themselves busy talking up their accomplishments.

The only fans who take my photos are DMV and surveillance cameras.

My memories are forgetful; they don't remember me.

Someone's always graduating from the campus of my dreams, leaving and not coming back.

I don't know who I am. I only see you watching.

If you open me, you'll find cypress leaves, the smell of traffic, the misquoted words of Hafez digesting with Cheerios, dates, and *naan*.

I'm a parasite, a marauder, a stranger waiting by the border to pen you down.

# Family of Scatterable Mines

Solmaz Sharif

Suitcases of dried limes, dried figs, pomegranate paste,
parsley laid in the sun, burnt honey, sugar cubes hardened
on a baking sheet. Suitcases of practical underwear,
hand-washed, dried on a door handle, stuffed into boxes
from Bazaar-e-Vakeel, making use of the smallest spaces,
an Arcoroc tea glass. One carries laminated prayers
for safe travel. I stand still when she smokes
esfand and fans away an evil eye. And when she asks
*does this mean he will die* I say yes
without worrying it will break her. Suitcases
of fruit knives, of embossed boxes
with gold coins inside, the gaudiest earrings
brought for me, yellow, loud as these big women rolling
meatballs on the kitchen floor, lifting lit coals
with their fingers onto a head of tobacco.
Shisha comes from shisheh, which means glass.
Jigaram, they call me, which means my liver.
Suitcases they unpack and repack
over Iranian radio, between calls passing gossip,
the report on the brother's liver: it's failing, and he
doesn't want the sisters around because they will pray
and cry over him like he's already dead,
which he will be in a few days, the one
who asked to read my poems. Sisters unfurl
black shawls from suitcases to drape over their heads.
I carry trays of dates before the men, offer little
square napkins, thank their condolences, hold the matriarchs
while they rock. I answered yes when one asked
*does that mean he's going to die?*

# Airport

GRANAZ MOUSSAVI

Search my bag.
        What's the use anyway?
The sigh hidden deep in my pocket
is all too familiar with: Halt!

Leave me alone!
        As a matter of fact, I'll sleep with the raspberry bush and
won't be faced down!
Why do you always target a woman
who abandons her walls,
        pins her heart to her shirt?
There's nothing in my suitcase
but innocent locks of hair.
        Leave me alone!

I dreamed I've stolen this heart from God,
and that I won't reach tomorrow.
I dreamed the place to which I'm going
my shoes stick to Friday.
What if God's land has Leukemia?

I'll tell my fortune with a dandelion, release its pedals to the moon:
come back Fridays of my childhood,
come back to me with that same boy
        whose hands sprouted kites
and I, with all my ten counting fingers,
        fell for him.
Why do you always target a women
who has pinned her heart to her shirt?

Here, in the bows and arrows of war's streets,
or in the muddied bellies of slack clotheslines,

the flights are always delayed.
The bats will eventually grow old.
At least give back my childhood photo.

Lonelier than a kite abandoned in a closet,
I am finally stamped, and I miss home.
The antenna shoots for the sky but
my dress on the clothesline embraces God.

*Translated by* Sholeh Wolpé

BLEEDING GREEN

# From Green to Green

SOHRAB SEPEHRI

I, in this darkness
wish for a luminous lamb
to come, to graze
on the grass of my weariness.

I, in this darkness
see my outstretched arms
wet beneath this rain
that once drenched
the first prayers of man.

I, in this darkness
opened doors
to ancient meadows,
to golden images we watched
on mythical walls.

I, in this darkness
saw the roots
and rendered
the meaning of water
to death's new sapling.

*Translated by* Sholeh Wolpé

# The Green of Iran

SHOLEH WOLPÉ

*For Iran's youth who have kept the Green Movement alive*

No departures here.
In Tehran out and in are closed,
under and over, stained.

Yet how green is the green of her sky.
The clouds bleed this green,
green the river, fields of rice,
the moss that grows
on Alborz mountain rocks.

The earth births this green
that the ants carry through
the cracks of Evin's* walls.
The birds shit green
on the turbans of bearded men.

Green is the green of this land,
the poplars lining parks,
green inked letters of lovers
holding hands in dark alleys
where green is the color of eyes,
the smell of dust swept clean.

Green is the ears of geraniums
on windowsills, and feet
of roses in backyards,
and the color of ponds
populated with green-

---

*Evin is Tehran's notorious prison in which political prisoners are held and tortured.

scaled fish, and frogs who sing
to the night dreams of green.

Protests following the 2009 Iranian presidential election against the disputed victory of Iranian President Mahmoud Ahmadinejad and in support of opposition candidate Mir-Hossein Mousavi occurred in major cities in Iran and around the world starting June 13, 2009. The protests were given several titles by their proponents including Green Revolution, Green Wave, or Sea of Green, reflecting presidential candidate Mousavi's campaign color, and also Persian Awakening.

# Song of a Forbidden Woman

GRANAZ MOUSSAVI

I have come
To tell about my breaths
You who breathe!
I have come
Body to body
To tell of the rope

Help me!
The stench of my stale voice takes my breath away
I have come
Help me
               Make a bridge with our bodies
Maybe I will remember my voice
I have come
Body to body
Panting
          To sing

But voices do not reach each other
              The rope separates
We do not reach each other
              The axe separates
My voice falls
And a green sigh echoes in the air

In my forbidden memory
The needle
         Scratches the voice of another woman:
           Something imploded in my body
         With the fall of our hands

Voices

Still dangle from branches
And it's not at all as if
Once again
Chairs and everything else have been removed
From below our voice boxes.

*Translated by* Niloufar Talebi

# At the Hamlet of Golestaneh

Sohrab Sepehri

How vast were the plains!
How high the mountains!
The scent of grass permeated Golestaneh!
I had gone there in search of something:
maybe slumber,
light, a pebble, a smile.

From behind the poplars
it was pure negligence calling me.

I paused by a field of reeds.
The wind blew, I listened.
Who was speaking to me?
A lizard skidded by.
I walked on,
past a hayfield,
a cucumber bed,
a blushing bush,
and the oblivion of earth.

On the lip of a stream
I slipped off my shoes
dipped my feet in the cool water:

*How green I feel today!*
*How sober is all my senses!*
*What if some sorrow is coming for me*
*from the other side of these mountains?*
*Who hides behind the trees?*
                    *No one. Just a grazing cow.*

*It's summer's high noon.*

*Shadows—those untainted*
*patches of bright purity—*
*know which summer this is.*

*Children of sensitivity! This is where you must play.*
*Life is not bleak:*
*there is kindness; there are apples; there is faith.*
*Yes,*
*one must live so long as there are poppies in bloom.*

*There is a presence in my chest,*
*like a dawn-spun dream,*
*a grove of light,*
*and I am so restless I want to run*
*to the limits of these plains,*
*past the top of these mountains.*
*Far in the distance a voice*
            *is calling my name.*

*Translated by* Sholeh Wolpé

# Summer Is a Green Story

ESTHER KAMKAR

One Day:
Mountain bluebirds
watch a thousand
humans step slowly
into a meadow
sit in silence
to see the sun rise.

Another Day:
Lock your cabin doors.
Bears awaken
in the Rockies.

One Day:
Green hands wave on the screen
green flags young green faces
forests of truncheons have risen
to crush and bury them.
How many fresh graves by sundown?

One Day:
Tuba Tree of Paradise
has its roots in the air,
nothing hidden there.

One More Day:
Green people
come from trees
human and leaf
fractals intersect
beeswax, color, heat
cover, then uncover

layers floating
translucent, fragile
memory molten
burnt in.

One Day Again:
Bend to grain
make a dwelling
a tent, a house
anywhere
after all
it is the same rock
same Sun, Moon, and Sky.
Love someone
give him the beehive
of your mouth.

# A New Idea

RUMI


Every dawn we rise out of the east
and shine like grains in the light.

We thrash about between wet and dry,
being neither one nor the other.

We hear what the brass objects want,
*Turn us into gold.*

To help with that we rise up into the stars.
We become pieces of amber on a necklace.
Our patched robes change to elegant apparel.
The world's poison turns to sweetness in us.

We move to the center of the fighting,
this circle of bewildered lovers.
We give the sign.
We knock at the placeless door,
riding a horse of green air.

Soul becomes pure in the body,
purer, we move inside love and stand next to Shams,
our shoulders touching in the infinite house.

*Translated by* Coleman Barks

# Feminist

MARYAM ALA AMJADI

I am a "woe-man"
And the man
Puts out
His cigarette of passion
Into my whole
I am a "woe-man"
And the man plants his heritage in me
I am a "woe-man"
And the man stands on my chest
And breathes deeply
I am a "woe-man"
And my name's Maryam
And I'm green
So so ever green
Things grow out of me
Love a baby a family
And a graveyard of serene doubts
And a blue blue silence
We are women
And the "you" in us
Could make such a fuss
For getting on the bus
That drives on the trail of Rights
And seizes the moments of might
In a siege of fright
We are women
And the "I" in you
Must see it through
The dark dark history tunnels
The light of injustice
That sounds so pathetic
So so tragic

We are women
we long haired
Short brained low intellect high heeled
We who share the "you" in "I"
And scratch out the "I" in "you"
We are the bad bad ones
in every every good
The women without a double "you"
Oh,
I am a woman!

# When a Color Stops Being a Color, Becomes Something Else Completely

SHIDEH ETAAT

Eighteen facing seats shining empty.
School is cancelled because men have
been hired to beat those wearing green,
to go inside dorm rooms smash computer screens
break beds turn trash bins upside down.
Where does one hide rebellion?

*It was imperative to have the leader's vision, and it was
announced then that his vision is this, that he elects Ahmadinejad.*

They have been told green is bad.
Green is the color of Allah-hatred.
They only take orders from their superior.
He is a man of good faith,
and so they believe him.
They are promised more money
than they make in a year.
Lunch will also be provided.

*The foundations of Islam and the foundations of Shi'ism and Velayat
are such that we have accepted the Velayat. When the Velayat has an
opinion,
everyone's opinion must follow, because if it's outside of this there is no
place for you. You're an outsider*

In Freedom Square notebooks under protesting arms,
bandanas cover warm mouths, foreheads glisten
from the sweat of remembering. Dark eyes.
Finely tweezed eyebrows. It is a sea of green.

*Over 18s went into one container and the under 18s into the several other*

*containers. The number of children under the age of 18 was greater.*
*They filled three or four containers of some 25 people in each.*

Old women with inflamed ankles the size of fists,
green veils cover their roots as they march, chanting
DEATH TO THE DICTATOR!
Even some of the clerics join, white cloth around heads,
hands rising to the air as if in conversation with God.
This is not what Allah meant at all.

*For illiterate people and those not able to complete their ballots, you*
*must do*
*so for them and complete them accordingly (for Ahmadinejad), no*
*matter*
*who their vote was intended for.*

Tear gas. Batons against bones buried
underneath skin. An eye desperate to shut.
It smells green, the air, as if the lentils
have sprouted, the goldfish are swimming
freely in bowls, as if spring has finally come.

*Sweets and pastries were offered and the forces were organized into*
*two shifts.*

Sidewalks are blood stained,
the air burning like someone's ashes.
A girl has been shot.
The protestors are running
the other way.

*I thought that I was continuing the path of my uncles and our martyrs.*

*All my interest and enthusiasm: to have the integrity for martyrdom.*

With chaos comes heartbreaking
slowness, loudness turning quickly into quiet.
The only thing heard,
the shaking of the fig tree leaves,
green, wild with
remembering.

All quotes are taken from "Iran: Basij Member Describes Election Abuse," by Linda Hilsum.

REBELLIOUS GOD

# Rebellious God

FORUGH FARROKHZAD

If I were God, I'd call on the angels one night
to release the round sun into the darkness's furnace,
angrily command the world garden servants
to prune the yellow leaf moon from the night's branch.

At midnight among the curtains of my divine palace,
I'd upturn the world with the frenzy of my furious fingers,
and with my hands, tired of their thousand-year stillness,
I'd stuff the mountains in the seas' open mouths.

I'd unbind the feet of a thousand fevered stars,
scatter fire's blood through the forests' mute veins,
rend the curtains of smoke so that in the wind's roar
fire's daughter can throw herself drunk into the forest's arms.

I'd blow into the night's magic reed
until the rivers rise from their beds like thirsty serpents,
and weary of a lifetime of sliding on a damp chest
pour into the dim marsh of the night sky.

Sweetly I'd call on the winds to release
the flower perfume boats on the rivers of night.
I'd open the graves so that myriad wandering souls
could once again seek life in the confines of bodies.

If I were God, I'd call on the angels one night
to boil the water of eternal life in Hell's cauldron,
and with a burning torch chase out the virtuous herd
that grazes in the green pastures of an unchaste heaven.

Tired of being a prude, I'd seek Satan's bed at midnight

and find refuge in the declivity of breaking laws.
I'd happily exchange the golden crown of divinity
for the dark, aching embrace of a sin.

*Translated by* Sholeh Wolpé

# Lovers!

TAHIRIH

Lovers! Creation veils his face no more!
Lovers, look! He himself is visible!

See! The face of God glows with glory:
Look, lovers! Bright, pure, blinding, beautiful!

Who made the cosmos turns earth green once more.
Rise! Rise from that dark so miserable!

The day of truth is here! Lies have turned to dust!
Order, justice, law are now possible.

Smashed, the despot's fist! God's hand opens:
grace pours down—not sorrow, pain, and trouble.

Minds in darkness now burn light with knowledge.
Tell the priest: Shut your book! Lock the temple!

Hatred and doubt once poisoned all the world.
The bloodied cup holds milk now—pure, ample!

Let nations hear who's come to set them free:
Broken the chain, and smashed the manacle!

*Translated by* Amin Banani

# Return to the Wellspring

JILA MOSSAED

*The world's territory, invisible, and the invisible world is the*
*fortress of the soul of life.*
—Pre-Islamic philosophical dictum

The crimson wind flings
dead locusts
to the cave dwellers' empty
meal place, caves hidden
       behind skyscrapers.
People have self-deceived
and scammed their made-up gods
so much that all they want sometimes
is to be truthful
in absolute godless
solitude.

Which suckling infant
       can vouch that milk tastes better in Sicily
or that in Baghdad docile
cows visit children
in their dreams to recount
true stories?
Silent sandstorms rain
on earth,
living aqueducts breathe
under busy thoroughfares.

I have drunk
from a bottomless jug
and walked on streets
where slave girls in white
rallied for future's freedom

I have seen slave boys running
on all fours and future-greedy
imposters who recorded
babble on the bark of date palms.*

Believe me
when the sand storm subsides
we will become little fish again
who in search of subterranean waters
will sink in the depths of sand.

---

*Koranic verses were written on the trunk of date palm trees 27 years after the prophet Mohammad's death.

# Criticizing the Veil

IRAJ MIRZA

She's wearing a veil, but still makes your heart melt with a glance;
God forbid that you should see her unveiled.

The city's Sheikh* scorns unveiling
because all his deceits are consummated under the veil.

Since what appears in the Qu'ran doesn't suit him,
he'll dig into the words and interpret them hypocritically.

One should never ask him for a reason
because a wolf will say anything to fool a lamb.†

Somebody posed a riddle, and I couldn't answer it,
but anybody who could is doing me a favor:

Aside from Iranians, what other creatures
would choose their mates without seeing them?

Why don't the masses of veiled women
rip the veils off their faces?

A woman's veiled face creates an obstruction to wisdom;
where's the hand of truth that should open this door?

Yes, the veil allows this group of Mufti‡
to rule like bosses over half of our people.

The Sheikh is stealthy like a cat in his piety;
no, the cat learns his tricks from the Sheikh.

*The Persian word *faghih* signifies one of the highest ranking clergy in the religious hierarchy.
†Here Iraj alludes to a famous Persian animal fable entitled "The Wolf and the Sheep."
‡A Mufti is a member of the ruling clergy who issues *fatawas*, or religious verdicts.

If the cat's paw gets a little wet,
he'll shake it wildly till it dries

holding his wet paw away from himself
like the city's Sheikh pretending to avoid impurity.

Anyone who's unaware of such a character flaw would think
the paw's wetness is torturing the cat.

However, when his insatiable eye spies a fish in the pond,
he'd jump headlong into the water up to his tail.

Don't be suspicious of me if I call you "Ms.";
watch out for the one who calls you "sister."

I'm in awe of how well the Sheikh mastered the secrets of hypnotism;
since he can transform a waking person into a sleeper.

Women on the Hajj all run around unveiled;§
tell the Sheikh to attack and wreck that house.

No one can catch the full moon's reflection in water
no matter how hard one tries.

You too should preserve your modesty while allowing your face to shine;
let the deceitful Sheikh remain howling like a dog.

We can't eradicate veils gradually
unless a revolution gives us a hand

---

§On the Hajj, women who visit Mecca are required not to wear a veil since at that time all fellow pilgrims are considered like brothers and sisters, close relations before whom a woman is not required to be veiled.

by tearing away the night's dark clouds
and illuminating streets and alleys with suns and moons.**

*Translated by* William Wolak *and* Mahmood Karimi-Hakak

---

**In Persian the words sun and moon are both feminine nouns and are frequently used as metaphors for a woman's beautiful face.

# Collage Sixteen

ZIBA KARBASSI

Before you launch your       red containership       on the frozen waters
Before you raise your sails       drink in the air full to its brim
The air is these few breaths of rain puttering down
Each breath a drop of rain       each one       a breath-drop of air
Close & kiss the eyes of jealous pasts goodbye
Those fleeting embraces that like a nap flip from the skull of your life
With those gulls that for your leaving bounce their wings against water
to say
                    their goodbye-betrayals, just say gurk-gurk to them
Empty out all strangers from the only one
In this self-war       until you come back to yourself       swear to
god       without god
                         that death always is certain
Stuff cotton into the ears of your godless captain
Tell them to tie your hands & feet to the ship's deck
I have sent my sirens out to bring you back
Don't be fullfooled by the magic of this poem
Breathing's a sparky fireball of colors       splashed by laughter

Hot garnet       warm cherry       soft pinks

Make your bones stronger
Go deep down deep
Down
To the depths

                         I'm so alone

*Translated by* Stephen Watts *and* Ziba Karbassi

# Martyrs of Iran

Roger Sedarat

In sacred ghazals martyrs of Iran
Die for verse. (They're all martyrs of Iran.)

The poet struck the beat upon his back;
His spiked belt buckled martyrs of Iran.

Though I pray for you, I'm far from dying.
It's impossible, martyrs of Iran.

Her name, "Neda," means voice. The whole world hears
Her silence. We're all martyrs of Iran.

Made-up American super heroes
Prove no match for real martyrs of Iran.

Killed with the Shah, my uncle's not among
True political martyrs of Iran.

Forget their sins in this transient world.
The spilled blood absolves martyrs of Iran.

Basiji kids buy toy Evin prisons
Where they torture doll-martyrs of Iran.

The thread of incense spelled Allah's ninety-
Nine names, linked to all martyrs of Iran.

One Aunt shows me dark bags under her eyes,
Another wrinkles . . . (martyrs of Iran)

Outside Iran, Ali reigns among best
Worst-death Karbala martyrs of Iran.

*Dear Roger,*

*We T'ank you for this poem*
*For our kids.*

*Love,*

*All Mot'ers of Iran.*

# I Didn't Ask for My Parents

SHOLEH WOLPÉ

It isn't like you bend
your dainty spirit neck
down from God's baby-soul-land
and point to a copulating couple
who strike your fancy.

Don't think it works that way.

You are blindfolded
and shot down through heaven's tunnel
into life and where you plop
willy-nilly that's your home.

The Jewish couple may be in the act
at the same time as their Muslim neighbor.

Where you end up
even the cherub who pushed you off
the edge can't know.

We grow up forgetting
our incidental placements
become fond of whatever
bread and religion we are fed.

Listen,

Who has salvation
when we all claim it?

# God's Poem

NADER NADERPOUR

Satan, O god of evil! You are indeed a poet.
Often have I envied your poetic flair.
You, who have created countless poems, are the true bard;
I, who have suffered many regrets, am the oblivious one.

"Love" and "gamble" are not God's poems, they are yours.
Such poetry is irresistible to all—all except
God, who would have neither, for no one remains
pious in "love" and in "gamble."

"Woman" with all her allure—your poetry!
"Woman" in her passionate creation—your verse!
"Wine" and "songs" are not to God's taste:
He forbad one to drink, and the other to hear.

You impart joy into kisses and glances,
you infuse delight into drunkenness and sin.
To those not enticed by God's afterlife Heaven,
you have flung open the gates to an earthly paradise.

For all your poems God may only have one,
but it's His masterpiece, His manifest miracle.
God's poem is *misery*— heart-filling,
satisfying sadness, and no more.

I know the poems you composed and He did not
—unless He penned others in someone else's name—
yet, if they place you and Him side by side,
which would you yourself prefer, tell me which?

*Translated by* Sholeh Wolpé

# Fire; take a step . . .

SEPIDEH JODEYRI

Saturday:
The newspapers will read:
That day
you will put your letters
in front of a gun
and then,
fire; take a step.
Sunday:
It's hot,
the sun
shoves us away
and we know by heart
the farthest color in the rainbow.
Fire; then a step.

Wednesday:
(The newspapers will read:)
It's hot,
and God
shoves us away.
It's as if your letters
see double;
as if
fourteen colors?!

Saturday:
It's hot,
the letters
shove us away.
Fire; then a step
towards the war!

*Translated by* Sholeh Wolpé

# Hezbollah

SHEEMA KALBASI

It is absurd to close your eyes
and pretend that the Bahá'ís
have never been slaughtered or forced
to convert to Islam,
as if the executions of political prisoners
or the Kurds were just part of a game,
an unwritten law in a lawless land.

Extended customs, mute prayers,
grave to grave, Tehran cemeteries
black from the flesh of the youth,
and on the faces of the mothers
chipped beliefs and spreading tears.

The News shows the Godzilla regime
—mourning over the tassels of demolished
homes of the homeless in a country
not even close to my land—sits on tinplates
of power and announces another castration.

This perhaps is a blessing from God
that when there is a Friday Prayer in Tehran,
we still cry over the Arab-Israeli War.

---

Hezbollah, which literally means Party of God, follows the distinctly Shiite Islamist ideology
developed by Ayatollah Ruhollah Khomeini, leader of the Islamic Revolution in Iran.
Bahá'ís are followers of the Bahá'í Faith, a global religion founded by Bahá'u'lláh in the nineteenth
century in Iran. It is the forbidden faith in post revolution Iran.

# A Homily on Leaving

NADER NADERPOUR

Look how these thugs have drained
God's dazzling divine word
from the spirit of love.

From here on everything you see
is the abandoned molts
of the cicada of words
that hang from the tree branches of speech.

Prophets of words!
You pen-wielding idols.
If your message was the Truth,
why did it crash like waves
at the shores of degradation?

Progeny of the shepherds who witnessed
the miraculous lightening of Moses
through the eyes of the Samaritans,
do you now take the rise of the golden calf
as a symbol of auspiciousness?
Perform your morning ablutions with new milk.
Pray for freedom.

And if your hopes, people,
are set upon the swallows' return,
turn away your gaze from the windows.
A new spring is not coming.

My longing was always this:
to be severed from this land.
I abandoned "I" so that I may
merge my words with God's.

Punish me, people,
if I be of the same stock as you.
If you are all curses,
it behooves me to be a prayer.
The Beloved's message will not come
from a foul mouth.

Blessed is the land of the conscious ones,
whose name I will not reveal;
blessed is the peal of melodies
in its twilight-hued sky.
I will go towards its spring
where roofs sprout green.
The scent of spring, friend,
cannot come from a swamp.

*Translated by* Sholeh Wolpé *and* Sahba Shayani

# Religion

AMY MOTLAGH

My father says: If she's so concerned, she can hire someone
to say them for her after she's gone. It's all the same
to God. He can't believe in the merit of children
reciting prayers for him after death, or in an afterlife
gotten to on tiptoe, across the razored filament
of truth. Still, he tried to bury her quickly,
in the white shroud prescribed by the religion, and he upheld
the Turkish coffee and the halvah, which we rolled
between our palms days after her death, waiting,
then ate it, the oily paste lining and closing
our throats at her graveside, where the showy gladiolus
and tea and dates marked us out again
against the green, clean-shaven American lawn,
and my father's cousin chanted the *fatiheh* in his place
just before the backhoe tamped soil into the hole
and the hired men folded sod over her grave.

# *Of Leaving*

SHOLEH WOLPÉ

Today's news is
wrapped around
tomorrow's dead fish.

Could it be that all windows
open to fiction while reality
burns in our stoves?

Time chimes in gods' bell towers,
and bottled sunlight gathers dust in caves
where humanity steeps in sour dreams of a savior.

Death is a bearded vagrant pushing a cartful
of lemon-yellow waning moons, and love is but a shadow
of itself, coreless and crumbling, like purity.

And God? God is always leaving, leaving
no footnotes to the commands He so lovingly leaves.

# STEPPING THROUGH TIME

# The Art of Stepping through Time

H. E. Sayeh

The world does not begin or end today
Sad and happy hide behind one curtain

If you're on the path don't despair of the distance
Arrival is the art of stepping through time

A seasoned traveler on the road to love's door
Your blood leaves its mark on every step

Still water soon sinks into the earth
But the river rolling grows into a sea

Let's hope that *one* reaches the target
So many arrows have flown from this old bow

Time taught me to fall out of love with your face
That's why these tears are tinted with blood

Pity this long game of decades
Plays the human heart as a toy

A caravan of tulips crossing this meadow
Was crushed underhoof by the riders of autumn

The day that sets spring's breath in motion
Will birth flowers and grasses from shore to shore

Mountain, you heard my cry today
The pain in this chest was born with the world

All praised brotherhood but did not live it
God, how many miles from tongue to hand?

Blood trickles my eyes in this corner of enduring
The patience I practice is squeezing my life

Come on, Sayeh, don't swerve from the path
A jewel is buried beneath every step

*Translated by* Mojdeh Marashi *and* Chad Sweeney

# In Praise of Big Noses

PERSIS KARIM

I am the only one of four sisters
who hasn't gone under the knife.
I resisted the pleas of my aunt and sisters
to become "more beautiful," "more you."
I've kept my stately proboscis
intact—choosing not to excise its grandeur.

It suits me, I suppose—evidence of my father,
those people who live in the drier, hotter climes
of the Mediterranean, in high desert plateaus,
cooling themselves with naso-thermo-regulation.
My old Jewish boyfriend used to say *how do the* goyim
*breathe from those things anyway?*

On my wedding day, my husband, also Jewish
and rather plentiful in that region of his face
completed his vows by saying "there is no guarantee in love,
but of this, I am certain: if we have a child he or she
will have a really big nose." When I nuzzle him
with mine, he pulls back his face, jumps

at the coldness of its tip. Contrary to popular belief, the nose
is not merely cosmetic—it can gauge temperature beyond the body.
And that's another thing, I've realized about the nose—
that smell is an underrated sense, perhaps a gift.
Imagine the possibilities for amplification: aromas
of jasmine, apple pie, saffron, lemon, rose,

might grow more intense, depending on the height
and angle of that fleshy mound. I admit to having no
scientific evidence for this, but I do wonder

what happens when a person alters
the things they were born with.

Whole industries were born from Iranian women
watching blonde, petite-nosed movie stars
who made them forget their own striking beauty
took thousands of years to evolve, only to be undone
by someone who decided that hairless, plucked, tucked,
sliced, nipped, and trimmed, were the loveliest
of them all. I like to think of the nose as great art
waiting to be discovered. Like those large-nosed kings
depicted on sides of temples, on papyrus, on caves, in colorful
Mayan pictographs like *Popul Voh*. Noses were signs
of nobility and prowess. Any king with a puny one
might have been thought of as small and impotent.

These days, I get a steady stream of e-mails offering penis
enlargement. But that's hidden, visible only
in bedroom interludes. The nose is the public display
of one's endowments—the relief map of a human face.
I study people's noses in order to read their origins—
to situate my gaze, to find how far out

in the world they really are.

# Untitled

Peyman Vahabzadeh

My father always said:
"Piss on all poetry;

             go after bread!"

I listened to the wisdom of that sage,
pissed on poetry
and went

          after bread.

Now
for thirty-five years
I've been eating bread

          that tastes like piss.

*Translated by* Sholeh Wolpé

# Those Who Stood Up for Tolerance

HAFEZ

May days of love's reunions be remembered,
May those days be remembered, may they always be remembered.

My mouth is poisoned by the bitterness of grief;
May the toasts of those happy drinkers be remembered.

Although my comrades are free from remembering me,
I remember them all constantly.

Though I'm captured and bound by this misery,
May the attempts of those who stood up for tolerance be remembered.

Even though a hundred rivers constantly flow from my eyes,
Zandehrud* irrigates for those who make gardens, may it be
remembered.

From now on the secret of Hafez will remain unspoken.
Have pity on those who must keep secrets; may that be remembered.

*Translated by* William Wolak *and* Mahmood Karimi-Hakak

---

*The Zandehrud is the main river that flows through Shiraz, the city of gardens.

# Rhyme by Rhyme

TAHIRIH

If I meet you face to face, eye to eye
my longing will unlace, strand by strand, sigh by sigh

Just to catch a glimpse of you, like a breeze I blow
house to house, door to door, lane to lane, by and by

In yearning, heart's blood gushes from my eyes
fountain by fountain, stream by stream, sea by sea, tide by tide

I wander the garden of your lips, cheeks, perfumed curls
blossom to blossom, tulip to tulip, scent to scent, vine to vine

I've been captured by your brows, eyes, even the mole on your face
trait by trait, love by love, kindness by kindness, stride by stride

This brooding heart weaves your love into her soul
stitch by stitch, thread by thread, warp by warp, guide by guide

Tahirih rummaged her heart and found only you, through and through
page by page, veil by veil, bend by bend, rhyme by rhyme

*Translated by* Sholeh Wolpé

# Stay Light on Your Feet

RUMI

Do you hear what the stringed instrument is saying?
I am long separated from a living body.

And this dry stick says, I was once part of a green branch.
Then a rider broke me off.

We are no different.
What we say is a caravan bell,
a cloud moving across.

Traveler, do not try to decide where to stop and live.
Whatever you are attracted to you weary of.

From being a sperm cell to a young man to an old man,
notice how you change.
Stay light on your feet and keep moving.

Speak any language, Turkish, or Greek, or Arabic,
but always speak love,
as wind rising off water tells about the river.
Follow my wake. Find a mirage that is real.

Learn from the moth what to do with fire.
The king has come into the city.
Why wander in ruins on the outskirts?

Take an oxwhip to your donkey.
Tenderness is not always appropriate.
Sometimes there must be sudden turning aside.

*Translated by* Coleman Barks

# Collage Eleven

ZIBA KARBASSI

As much as I try to run from death-ness, my height doesn't suit
life's patience
Patience
Has the aura of dropsy rain
Stiffened downpours of risk & un-worry
And calloused fingers don't know how to      how to in this dank dark
Put right my hat      or      yellow-shiny coat of rain      over my head
When the only pearl of rain is not my pearl
In this shot-earth      his breath is not here
And I am not      earth-less      I'm breath-less
In this short-voice      not even breath breathes      between walking feet
I cannot walk      straight into this poem
I can't grow taller
When he is not shore      I cannot sea
On the metal nerves of this town      no instrument of music can play me
Under infected teeth      my feet start to break-dance
As much as I try to run away from death-ness my height doesn't fit with
life's patience
As much as I try to chrysalis myself from this mausoleum
Always the collapsing walls are too tardy for my head
As much as I try to gulp in this sea      salt of its salt      I becalm
My feet run away from me      I dwindle into the distance
The lessen of my life      always the diminished me
Leave me be
I have wasted away
Death      death is most welcome
Only in the embrace of my grave      engrave this: I had only his embrace
less in this life

*Translated by* Stephen Watts *and* Ziba Karbassi

# Collage Fourteen

ZIBA KARBASSI


When it's all over
Behind your head there's empty air
In front of you        from whatever is & is not        also more or less air
When your        breath starts finger-snapping        you won't crack up
When your breath starts back-flipping        it'll hopscotch & hip-hop
in mid-air
Where's your mind gone to!
When contracts & clauses cuddle up to the Koran        the soul becomes
                                            shoddy


Exams        are to be retaken        over again
When you're not seen        how can you hear
Veils of music make bloody        wounds winding & waving as air
Vocabularies that fall from such waves are so well-crafted!
Give wings to the fish that when they dance
They'll gill-open & close up again        like winking light-houses
Dancing is a river        when it flows with words it will reach        the sea


Give skyscrapers wings
That they shall graze skies        then fall to your hand & swim in your palm
The square that jumps from its cube        was in love
In the rounds of becoming a circle        scalping her head on all the walls
And blood was breaking from all her edges        and she was laughing
It is when the mouth laughs that it burns


That full-stop stopped in my belly        is my belly-button
Come down just a little
No, not there        come to my eyes
Come back to my eyes


*Translated by* Stephen Watts *and* Ziba Karbassi

# The Plumber's Poem

ZARA HOUSHMAND

That's my hair that's wrapped around your snake, Ben Yakov.
It's filthy, but it's mine.
Seventy-nine dollars and fifty cents.
A plumber earns more than a writer does,
and we both laugh.
I don't mind, write the check.

My name? Iran,
I mumble.
Your accent undresses Israel.
Our eyes meet, apologize,
just you and I
for history
for all the politicians' lies
and for the real things too.
The unspeakable things.

Are you happy? I ask,
but really I'm asking
What do you miss?
(Green almonds and the smell of kerosene;
the language of my dreams.)
But you say Yes, and anyway,
where else could I go?

# My Hands Tremble Yet Again—A Soliloquy

SHEIDA MOHAMMADI

When
the sky
pulls its coat tight over its head, and
the rain keeps nagging, and
my pink doll
misses the sun . . .
I become weary of you.

When
the teacup on the table
is a crow staring at me
my throat begins to taste like caw caw.
Black-beaked clock

until dawn

black-beaked clock

till dawn

Clock . . .
The telephone goes mad with silence,
and I, go blue with you.

Aromas quit the house.
Happiness ditches me.
And the dirty laundry
keeps spinning, spinning . . .

My mother's silver spoons drift and dash in the kitchen. Unironed shirts
lounge over cactus trees. I put on your dirty socks and waltz
with your black striped pants. The house spins around this washing
machine, round my head. Dirty dishes play games on the kitchen floor.
I yell at the flower pots and blow out the candles. Happy birthday to
me!

I bang on the typewriter and am drenched in your hands' dried up
sweat.
I change the TV channel to coax a yawn into my swollen lids.
I hate the pink nail polish bottle I found on the piano.

Black-beaked clock
                    until dawn
Black-beaked clock
                    till dawn
        clock . . . .
Now
the sycamore's yellow bluffs
and highway 118 . . .
don't pass me by.

Strawberries,
like your expressions of love,
make me want to barf.
This month,
that month,
I come to hate you.
I hate you.

*Translated by* Sholeh Wolpé

# Hot Tea, a Warm Muffin

SHIDEH ETAAT

You have forgotten the simplest of things—
like our names,
what year it is,
or that you were once married to a man
you did not love,
but spent your life with anyway.

Some days you are a curious child,
others, an old woman ready to die.

And some days you are my grandmother,
who sits at the café
and asks if I'm cold,
if I've fallen in love
yet.

This is all that is left for you—
hot tea, a warm muffin,
and our familiar hands ready
to feed you the only sweetness left.

And somehow,
even though you can't tell me
how long we have been here for,
you can sit in this chair and say,
*I am sitting in the greatest place of all.*

# Mulberries and Chador

FARZANEH MILANI


She would spread her chador
under the mulberry tree, and gently
hit the branches with a long pole.

Sitting on the edge of her cotton chador
I thought my grandmother was a magician.
Giddy with joy I'd watch

the mulberries drift and dance
like fattened snowflakes
into my cupped receiving hands.

Harder, grandma, I would plead,
hit harder, and she'd laugh, and say,
"We can't hurt pregnant trees,"

and twirl her wand into its blizzard
of decades, oceans I've yet to travel
beyond the hem of her mulberry-studded dreams.

# Return from My Body's Black-and-Blue

SHEIDA MOHAMMADI

Leeches, kindly leeches suck my blood
and the crane, heavy-handed crane
lifts my corpse up from the pit,
with my skull full of snowy days.

Leeches, kindly leeches
blacken my body
you return from my body blues
hitting your head against your hands!

Save your teardrops for me, love.
I have run head-on into myself, crashed into myself
and the road's searchlights have dumped me onto this lake's floor.
Look at how black I appear in your smoke-colored sunglasses!
And these women
look how they hide my breasts under their chadors.

Save your teardrops for me, love.
Why do you, so pale and fair, arrive so late?
And why has my son, so little
swelled so much inside me in the few months of my pregnancy?
And the leeches—kind leeches
Look how they suck my blood. . . .

*Translated by* Ahmad Karimi-Hakkak

# Caravan

H. E. SAYEH

It's late, Galia!
Don't sing a love story in my ear!
And don't ask for passionate ghazals!
It's late, Galia, the caravan has started to move

Our love for each other? . . . Yes,
That's a story, too,
But as long as our people grope for the night's bread
There's no time for stories or romance

Blooming on the twilight of your birthday
Your glow lights twenty candles
Yet the same night a thousand girls your age
Sleep hungry and naked on the ground

While the dance and tease of your fingers
Move beautifully over sitar strings
A thousand weaver girls
With bloody, infected fingers
Die slowly, the soul unraveling from the body
In the tight cage of the workshop
For less pay than you would toss to a beggar's lap

And this seven-color carpet crushed beneath your dance
Has earned its prism from the blood of human beings
In the warp and weft of each line and figure: a thousand sufferings
In the design of each flower and leaf: a thousand shames

Here a thousand innocent hopes have slept buried in earth
And the wind has swept a thousand young fires

Here the hands of a thousand blameless children
The ruined eyes of a thousand sick girls . . .

It's late, Galia!
This is no time for kisses and love poems
Everything has the color of fire and blood
It's the revolution of voices and hands
It's the revolution of life

Don't smile in my face!
From now on your gaze
Is forbidden—so is wine and love!
And the drumming of a happy heart!

My friends are bound in wet dark
Dungeons at the Shah's palace
In fevered exile at Khark Island
At each edge and corner of this black hell

It's early, Galia!
Don't sing a love story in my ear!
And don't ask for songs of passion
It's early, Galia! The caravan has not arrived . . .

The same day the pearled arms of dawn
Swing a scimitar to tear the night's curtain,
The day the sun
Flickers through each crack in the wall
And the cheeks of war-tired friends
Find again the colors of laughter
I'll be back on that day

To songs and ghazals and kisses
To the fertile, heart-thawing spring
And to you

       my love

*Tehran, 1952*

*Translated by* Mojdeh Marashi *and* Chad Sweeney

# Connection

FORUGH FARROKHZAD

The black of my irises,
those simple, reclusive Sufis of mine
swooned in the song-spell of his eyes.

I sensed him billow all around me,
radiating towards infinity
to the other side of life
like fire's red pyramid,
like a cloud in spasm of rain,
like a sky embraced
by warm seasons' breath.

I sensed that in the breeze
of his hands' movements
the substance of my being
was disintegrating.
I sensed his heart peal inside mine
like the bell of a wandering sorcerer.

The clock took flight.
The curtain withdrew with the wind.
I had pressed him to myself
inside the halo of that fire
and I wanted to say something
but to my astonishment
his thick shadowing lashes
released themselves like silk strands
from the base of darkness
along desire's long trail
and through the tremor
—that deathly tremor—
to the end of my end.

I sensed my release.
I sensed my release.

I sensed my skin crack from love's dilating joy,
as my flaming mass melted slowly
and flowed, streamed and flowed
into the moon,
a turbulent blurry moon
drowned in a ditch.

We had cried into each other.
We had madly lived a moment's
ephemeral union inside one other.

*Translated by* Sholeh Wolpé

# I Won't Quit Loving

HAFEZ

I won't quit loving the friend and wine.
Hundreds of times I repented, but never again.
Garden of Eden, creation's tree, and even virgins of paradise
Can't compare with dirt from the friend's alleyway.

Lectures and homework instilling knowledge contain only a hint;
I just gave you an aside, and I'm not about to repeat myself.

I'm never aware of what's going on inside my head
Until it rises above everyone in the middle of the tavern.

Sarcastically the teacher said, "Abandon loving."
There's no need quarreling, brother; I just won't stop.

This much virtue is enough for me-
That I don't flirt with the city's beauties from the pulpit.

Hafez, the guide's living presence dispenses real wealth;
I'll never stop kissing the dirt beneath such feet.

*Translated by* William Wolak *and* Mahmood Karimi-Hakak

# *Morning Star*

ZIBA KARBASSI

all these stars but
        only one star to hook on the black
                of her skirt

and it rips that skirt wide open
        it rips the skirt of the night wide
              open

and then
        little by little the red
            and then little by
                little red-orange
            and then little
                by little orange yellow
            and then little
                by little the yellow
                  milk

and when night passes out to neurosis,
            the colors erupt
and it pushes itself up and up and down and up,
        night, with all its nervous
            energy

     here, right here
        in front of us

        but

when the first slit of sunlight slants across us

any star, any single star can
be the morning
one

*Translated by* Stephen Watts *and* Ziba Karbassi

# Twittering

PEGAH AHMADI

We lower our heads to our chests
sunshine falls off the swing,
we raise the swing to our chests
it falls off the frame.

I have never been so much a child!
With my voice unaccompanied by the sound of Kamancheh!
I have never climbed to the moon through the alley,
have never reached the bottom of my childhood with a sigh!
And that's the tepid reason
on this unique night
why the wheat sheaf of my hair is tied to your dreams!

Come up one more rooftop
higher than this mouth that breathes through your boots
higher than this air that ties its vein to the moon!

Stretch your feet through the sky behind me
I feel sleepy, Cotton!
I feel sleepy!
and my sleep keeps delaying my birth, come on!

Last night, from among all the afflicted nights up on the moon
no city had been left along the way
except for my soaked land.
Tonight, I am the whole of this shoreless sky
and night pulsates in my temples
its stairs lost.
And all that's left of the heart is a man
who "passes by the wet trees."*

---

*The phrase is from a long lyrical poem by Forugh Farrokhzad, titled "Let's Believe in the Dawn of the Cold Season" (see *Sin: Selected Poems of Forugh Farrokhzad*, University of Arkansas Press).

I have never been so much in love
Never been so beautiful
Never been so much a poet.

And my heart is this very poem
that comes "along the wet trees."
and I have no doubt
that my most chest-cherished memory will be
this very thing,
this twittering!

*Translated by* Ahmad Karimi-Hakkak

# Someone like No One

FORUGH FARROKHZAD

I dreamed someone's coming.
I dreamed of a red star.
My eyelids keep jumping
and my shoes keep pairing.
Blind me if I lie.

I dreamed of that red star
when I was awake. I saw
someone's coming.
Someone's coming.
Someone different.
Someone better.
Someone like no one.
Not like father,
not like Ensi,
not like any man,
not like Yahya,
not like mother.
Someone like one should be,
taller than the trees by the architect's home,
and his face
even brighter than Imam Mehdi's.
He's not afraid of Siyyid Javad's brother
—who's gone and put on a police uniform—
not even afraid of Siyyid Javid himself
who owns every room of our house.
And his name, as mother says
in the beginning and the end of her prayers,
is either *Judge of Judges*
or *Granter of Wishes.*

And he can recite,

with eyes closed,
all the hard words
in the third-grade book;
he can even subtract a thousand from twenty million
and not come up short.
He can buy everything he needs
from Siyyid Javad's shop on credit;
and can make the Allah lamp
that used to shine green like dawn;
light up again in Moftahian mosque's sky.

Oooh . . .
How nice light is.
How nice light is.
And how I wish
Yahya had a cart
and a kerosene lamp
so I could sit on his cart
among the watermelons and cantaloupes
and ride around the Mohmadieh square.

Oooh . . .
What fun riding around the square.
What fun sleeping on the roof.
What fun going to the City Park.
How great the taste of Pepsi.
How nice is Fardin Cinema.
How I love all good things,
and how I'm dying to yank
Siyyid Javad's daughter's braids.

Why am I so small

that I get lost in the streets?
Why doesn't father— who isn't small
and doesn't get lost in the streets—
do something to hurry the arrival
of the one I've dreamed of?
Or the folks who live in the slaughterhouse district,
whose garden soil is blood soaked,
whose pond water is blood streaked,
and whose shoes trace blood . . .
Why don't they do something?
Why don't they do something?

How lazy is the winter sun.

I swept the stairs to the roof,
washed the window panes too.
Why does father dream only when he sleeps?

I swept the stairs to the roof,
washed the window panes too.

Someone's coming.
Someone's coming.
Someone whose heart is with us,
whose breath is with us,
whose voice is with us.

Someone whose coming can't be stopped, handcuffed, and thrown in jail.
Someone who's had babies under Yahya's old trees
and is getting bigger and bigger
day by day.
Someone's coming from the rain, from the sound of pouring rain,

from among the whispering petunias.

Someone's coming from the sky over the artillery field, on fireworks' night.
And he'll spread the tablecloth,
and divide the bread,
and divide the Pepsi,
and divide the City Park,
and divide the whooping-cough syrup,
and divide the school registration day,
and divide the hospital numbers,
and divide the rubber boots,
and divide Fardin Cinema,
and divide Siyyid Javad's daughter's clothes,
and everything else that's left,
and give us our share too.
I dreamed . . .

*Translated by* Sholeh Wolpé

# Water

Sohrab Sepehri

Let's not muddy the water:
Down yonder, a pigeon drinks.
In a far away thicket, a finch bathes.
In a village somewhere, a jug is filled.

Let's not muddy the water:
perhaps it flows towards a poplar
to wash away the sorrow from a heart,
or to the foot of a dervish who dips in his bread.

A beautiful woman has come to the stream's edge.
Her reflection repeats her beauty.
Let's not muddy the water.

How lucent the stream!
How sweet the water!
How the folks up yonder savor!
May their springs surge.
May their cows give abundant milk.

Though I've never been
to that village, I know
God's footsteps grace its fields.

The moon there spreads her light
on their talk, and no doubt
their clay walls are low.
The people of that village know
what poppies are.
No doubt there, blue is blue,
and when a flower blooms
the whole village is aware.

What a township!
May its streets overflow with song!

Those on the stream's edge understand the water.
They have not muddied it.
Let us too not muddy the water.

*Translated by* Sholeh Wolpé

# About the Poets and Translators

Pegah Ahmadi was born in Tehran. She began writing poetry at the age of seven. At seventeen she made her début as a poet by the publication of a poem in the literary magazine *Takāpu*. Since then she has regularly contributed to literary magazines inside Iran. She is the author of four books of poetry.

Ahmad Reza Ahmadi was born in 1940 in Kerman, Iran. He is the author of thirteen books of poetry.

Maryam Ala Amjadi is an Iranian poet and translator. She is the author of two collections of poems, *Me, I and Myself* (2003) and *Gypsy Bullets* (2010). She was awarded a silver medal in the 14th National Persian Literary Olympiad (2001), and an honorary fellowship in creative writing at the International Writers Program at the University of Iowa (2008). Her literary translations include a selection of Raymond Carver's poetry, *Fear of Arriving Early,* which she translated from English into Persian (2009). She currently lives in Pune, India.

Ali Alizadeh was born in Iran in 1976 and migrated to Australia at fourteen. He began writing in English in his late teens and received his PhD in professional writing from Deakin University, Melbourne. His books include the collection of poetry *Eyes in Times of War* (2006) and the novel *The New Angel* (2008). His latest book is a work of creative nonfiction titled *Iran: My Grandfather* (2010). The poem "Marco Polo," included in this anthology, is from Alizadeh's forthcoming collection of poetry *Ashes in the Air* (2011).

Amin Banani is professor emeritus of history and Persian literature at the University of California, Los Angeles. He is the author of *Mysticism and Poetry in Islam: The Heritage of Rumi* (1987) and *Persian Literature* (1988).

REZA BARAHENI was born in Tabriz, Iran, in 1935. He is a poet, literary translator, critique, and novelist who spent time in prison for his writings during the Shah's regime and later, in the early years of the Islamic Republic's government. He is the author of more than fifty books in both Persian and English, and his works have been translated into dozens of languages. The poems in this book first appeared in translation in *God's Shadow: Prison Poems* (1976).

COLEMAN BARKS was born in 1937 in Chattanooga, Tennessee. Since 1977 he has collaborated with various scholars of the Persian language (most notably, John Moyne) to bring to American free verse the poetry of the thirteenth-century mystic, Jalaluddin Rumi. This work has resulted in twenty-one volumes (including the bestselling *Essential Rumi* in 1995), two appearances on Bill Moyers' PBS specials, and inclusion in the prestigious *Norton Anthology of World Masterpieces*. The Rumi translations have sold more than a million copies.

KAVEH BASSIRI is the cofounder of Triptych Readings, which presents established and emerging poets, and the literary arts director of Persian Arts Festival, which runs a monthly poetry reading at Bowery Poetry Club in New York City. He is the recipient of the 2010 Witter Bynner Poetry Translation Residency. His writing won the Bellingham Review's 49th Parallel Award and was recently published in *Virginia Quarterly Review, Drunken Boat, Free Verse, Harpur Palate,* and *Mississippi Review* in which his poem "Memorial Day" (2010) was first published.

SIMIN BEHBAHANI is a distinguished voice in Iranian literature. She is the author of numerous books of poetry and essays. Her work has attracted the attention and admiration of an ever-growing readership inside and outside Iran. Her poems in this collection first appeared in *A Cup Of Sin: Selected Poems* (1999).

MOHSEN EMADI was born in Sari, Iran, in 1976. He is the author of a collection of poetry, *The Flower of the Lines,* translated into Spanish and published in Spain. He is the founder and manager of Ahmad Shamlou's official website and the House of World Poets website, a Persian anthology of world poetry that includes the works of more than 100 modern poets.

SHIDEH ETAAT is a graduate student in the professional writing program at the University of Southern California. She lives in Los Angeles.

FORUGH FARROKHZAD was born in 1935 in Tehran, Iran. Her poetry was the poetry of protest—protest through revelation— of the innermost world of women (a taboo subject until then), their intimate secrets and desires, their sorrows, longings, aspirations, and at times even their articulation through silence. On February 14, 1967 she died in a car crash. She was 32 years old. All translations of her poems in this collection (except "Connection") are from *Sin: Selected Poems of Forugh Farrokhzad* (2007). A translation of "Connection" first appeared in and was commissioned by *Words without Borders.*

HASSAN FAYYAD is an alumnus of UCLA's film school and former writer-director of documentary films for the Iranian Ministry of Culture and Arts. He has translated two collections of poems into Persian: *Freedom: Selected Poems by Octavio Paz* and *Homesick Blues: Selected Poems of Langston Hughes.*

HAFEZ was born in Shiraz, Iran, circa 1320 and died around 1390. Not much is known about his life except the most general facts. The son of a merchant, Hafez was well educated, married, and had a son. After his talent for poetry was recognized, Hafez became the court poet for most of Shiraz's rulers who reigned during his lifetime. The translations of his poems in this collection first appeared in *Your Lover's Beloved: 51 Ghazals by Hafez* (2009).

MARYAM HOOLEH was born in Tehran, Iran, in 1978 to a Kurdish family. She illegally left Iran in 1997, and in Greece she published her second volume of poetry, *In the Alleys of Athens* (1999), which was later published in Iran in a censored version. In 2001 she was invited to Sweden by Iranian Women's Studies Foundation where she published her third volume of poems, *Cursed Booth*, which won her a Swedish PEN fellowship in 2003. Her other books include *Inferno Inc.*, *Leprosy Now, Kites Will Never Fly Away in My Hands,* and *The Sticky Dreams of a Banished Butterfly*. The translation of her poem in this collection first appeared in *Belonging: New Poetry by Iranians Around the World* (2008). Hooleh presently lives in Sweden.

ZARA HOUSHMAND is an Iranian-American writer who lives in Austin, Texas. Her work includes poetry, theater, virtual reality, literary translation, and editing the Mind & Life Institute dialogues between the Dalai Lama and scientists. Her poetry has been published in both online and print literary journals. Her most recent book is *A Mirror Garden* (2007), a memoir coauthored with Monir Farmanfarmaian.

ROGER HUMES is a poet and a computer graphic artist. He is the director of The Other Voices International Project, a cyber-anthology of world poetry, and the international poetry editor for *Harvest International*, an annual arts and literature magazine produced by the California State Polytechnic University, Pomona. He lives in Claremont, California.

SEPIDEH JODEYRI was born in 1976 in Ahvaz, Iran. She has written poems and short stories since she was seven and as a professional author since 1997. She has published two collections of poems, *Dream of the Amphibious Girl* (2000) and *Some Pink Inclined to my Blood* (2007), , and a collection of short stories, *Logical* (2001). She also has translated a selection of Edgar Allan Poe's works and a selection of Jorge Luis Borges's poems into Persian.

SHEEMA KALBASI was born in 1972 in Tehran, Iran. She is an award winning poet, producer, blogger, and human rights advocate. She is the founder and president of Reel Content, a film production and publishing company, and the director or codirector of several literary projects including the Other Voices International Project. She has published two books of poetry and two anthologies of poems.

ESTHER KAMKAR is the author of a full length collection of poems, *Hummingbird Conditions* (2002), and a chapbook, *A Leopard in My Pocket* (1998). Born in Tehran, Iran, she currently resides in Northern California.

ZIBA KARBASSI was born in Tabriz in northwestern Iran. She had to leave her country with her mother in the mid-1980s and for most of the time since then she has lived in London. She has published seven books of poetry. She was chairperson of the Iranian Writers Association (in exile) from 2002 to 2004 and editor of *Asar* and *Exiled Ink* literature magazines in London. Her poems have appeared in many languages throughout Europe and the United Kingdom.

PERSIS KARIM is the editor of *Let Me Tell You Where I've Been: New Writing by Women of the Iranian Diaspora* (2006) and coeditor of *A World Between: Poems, Short Stories and Essays by Iranian-Americans* (1999). Her poetry has been published in numerous print and online literary journals. She is the founder of the Association of Iranian American Writers and teaches English and comparative literature at San Jose State University.

MAHMOOD KARIMI-HAKAK is professor of creative arts at Siena College. He has created more than fifty stage and screen productions in the United States, Europe, and his native Iran, and has received four artistic and scholarly awards including the Fulbright (2009). His literary credits include six plays, two books of poetry, several translations from and into Persian, and numerous articles and interviews in English and Persian. His Hafez cotranslations in this anthology are from *Your Lover's Beloved: 51 Ghazals by Hafez* (2009).

AHMAD KARIMI-HAKKAK is a professor and founding director of the Roshan Cultural Heritage Institute Center for Persian Studies in the School of Languages, Literatures, and Cultures at the University of Maryland. Karimi-Hakkak is the author of nineteen books and more than one hundred major scholarly articles.

ESMAIL KHOI was born in 1938 and is the author of many collections of poetry. He was educated in Iran and England, and began his career in Iran as a lecturer in philosophy. In the 1960s and '1970s, as a founding member of the Writers Association of Iran, he opposed the restrictions placed on intellectual freedoms in monarchial Iran, gradually advocating revolutionary change.

SHAMS LANGEROODI was born in 1951, in Langrood, Iran, a coastal town edging on the Caspian Sea. In 1981, he was arrested as a political activist and served a six-month sentence due to his opposition. He has published six collections of poetry, including *Notes for a Warden Nightingale* and *The Hidden Celebrations*, a novel, a play, and an anthology of Iranian poetry. His four-volume history of modern Iranian poetry, *Analytical History of the New Poetry*, was banned in Iran for many years. The poem "From '23' printed in this collection was first commissioned and printed online by Words without Borders.

MOJDEH MARASHI is a San Francisco Bay Area writer, designer, and visual artist. Marashi earned a master of arts in interdisciplinary arts and will finish her master's degree in creative writing from San Francisco State University in 2010. Her translations of Sayeh's works (with Chad Sweeney) have appeared in *Crazyhorse, Indiana Review, Poetry International, American Letters & Commentary, Seattle Review, Subtropics,* and *Washington Square.*

FARZANEH MILANI teaches Persian language and literature and women's studies at the University of Virginia and is the author of *Veils and Words: The Emerging Voices of Iranian Women.*

IRAJ MIRZA (JALALU'L-MAMALEK) was born in 1874 in Tabriz, Iran. His fluency in French and Russian and his trip to Europe deepened two of his unshakeable beliefs: that Iran needed to modernize and that a crucial part of that modernization process included the emancipation of women. He died at the age of 52 on March 14, 1926.

SHEIDA MOHAMMADI was born in Tehran, Iran, and received her bachelor of arts in Persian language and literature from Tehran University in

1999. Author of three books, she was recognized by the Encyclopedia Britannica as one of the most notable contemporary Persian writers of 2010. Her third book, *Aks-e Fowri-ye Eshqbazi (The Snapshot of Making Love)* was published in 2007. Her poems have been translated into different languages, including English, French, Turkish, Kurdish, and Swedish.

JILA MOSSAED was born in Iran in 1948 and has been living in Sweden since 1986. She is the author of eight volumes of poetry and two novels in Persian, four volumes of poetry in Swedish, and one in Spanish, as well as numerous political articles. She is the recipient of a number of literary awards in Sweden.

AMY MOTLAGH currently lives in Egypt, where she is an assistant professor in the Department of English and Comparative Literature at the American University in Cairo.

GRANAZ MOUSSAVI, born in 1974 in Tehran, Iran, is an award winning poet and film maker. She is the author of four books of poetry and is currently completing her doctorate in poetic cinema at the University of Western Sydney in Australia. The translation of "Song of a Forbidden Woman" first appeared in *Belonging: New Poetry by Iranians Around the World* (2008).

NAANAAM (HOSSEIN MARTIN FAZELI), born in June 1964 in Shiraz, Iran, is an Iranian-Canadian film director and poet. He is the author of four collections of poetry in Persian and his films have won thirty-nine international awards.

NADER NADERPOUR was born on June 6, 1929, in Tehran, Iran. He was a nominee for the Nobel Prize in Literature, and a 1993 recipient of the Human Rights Watch Organization's Hellman-Hammett Grant (awarded to writers in exile whose works are banned in their own homelands). He died in exile February 18, 2000.

PARTOW NOORIALA was born in Tehran, Iran. She is the author of five books of poetry, a collection of critiques, and a collection of short stories.

SHIRINDOKHT NOURMANESH was born and raised in Tehran, Iran. Her first collection of short stories and novellas, *Domal (The Abscess)*, was published in the United States, and her translations, stories, and memoirs have appeared in print and online journals.

TAHIRIH (QURRATU'L-'AYN) is a controversial woman in Iranian history. A poet, activist, scholar, and mystic, she converted to the Ba'bi faith and was known as the first woman to remove her veil in the company of men. In 1852, she was murdered for her beliefs and her condemnation of clergy and state. The translation of her poem "Lovers!" was first published in *Tahirih: A Portrait in Poetry* (2004).

YADOLLAH ROYAI was born in Damqan, Iran, in 1931. He is a well-known poet of post-revolutionary Iran. Shortly after the 1979 revolution he immigrated to France where he continued to write and publish.

RUMI, also known as Molana, was born in 1207 in the present day Afghanistan and died in 1273. The *Christian Science Monitor* ranked the thirteenth-century Persian lawyer-divine and Sufi America's best-selling poet in 1997. His followers founded the Sufi Order of the Whirling Dervishes.

KAVEH SAFA has taught courses in anthropology and Persian at the Universities of Virginia and Chicago.

H. E. (HOUSHANG EBTEHAJ) SAYEH was born in 1927 in the city of Rasht in northern Iran. His work emphasizes current issues of Iranian society, especially the national crises which followed the coup d'état of 1953 and the Revolution of 1979. He is the author of twelve collections of poetry and lives alternately in Germany and Iran.

ROGER SEDARAT won the Ohio University Press Hollis Summers Poetry Prize with his first poetry collection, *Dear Regime: Letters to the Islamic Republic*. He teaches poetry and translation in the master of fine arts program at Queens College, City University of New York.

Sohrab Sepehri was born in 1928 in Kashan, Iran. A gifted painter and poet, Sepehri draws his images from eastern mysticism. His first volume of poetry, *Death of Colors*, was published in 1951; however he did not come to prominence until the publication of his third book, *Water's Footfall*, in 1965. He published three more volumes of poetry while exhibiting his paintings in galleries around the world. He died of blood cancer in 1980 at the Pars Hospital in Tehran.

Ahmad Shamlou was born in 1925 in Tehran, Iran. A gifted early modernist poet and a follower of Nima Yushij, Shamlou went on to develop his own distinct style. He published more than twenty volumes of poetry. Today, he is a highly revered literary figure in modern Iranian history.

Solmaz Sharif was born in Istanbul, Turkey. She holds degrees from the University of California, Berkeley, where she studied and taught with June Jordan's Poetry for the People, and New York University, where she was a Goldwater Fellow. Her work has appeared or is forthcoming in *jubilat*, *Diagram*, and PBS's *Tehran Bureau*. She is currently the managing director of The Asian American Writers' Workshop.

Sahba Shayani is a graduate student of Iranian studies at the University of California, Los Angeles, where he is currently working on a doctorate in Persian language and literature. He received his bachelor of arts in English and his master of arts in Iranian studies, at the same university.

David St. John has written several books of poetry, including *The Face: A Novella in Verse* (2005); *Prism* (2002); *In the Pines: Lost Poems* (1999); *Study for the World's Body: New and Selected Poems* (1994), which was nominated for the National Book Award; *Terraces of Rain: An Italian Sketchbook* (1991); *No Heaven* (1985); *The Shore* (1980); and *Hush* (1976). He is also the author of a volume of essays and interviews, *Where the Angels Come Toward Us* (1995).

Chad Sweeney is the author of three books of poetry: *Parable of Hide and Seek* (2010), *Arranging the Blaze* (2009), and *An Architecture* (2007). He is also the editor of *Days I Moved Through Ordinary Sounds* (2009).

His poems have appeared widely, including in *Best American Poetry* and *Verse Daily*.

Niloufar Talebi was born in London to Iranian parents. She is the founding director of The Translation Project, the editor/translator of BELONGING: *New Poetry by Iranians Around the World* (2008), and the creator/performer of multimedia pieces *Four Springs* (2004), *Midnight Approaches* (2006), ICARUS/RISE (2007), and *The Persian Rite of Spring* (2010).

Peyman Vahabzadeh is an assistant professor of sociology at the University of Victoria. He received his Ph.D. in sociology from Simon Fraser University in the summer of 2000 and recently completed his post-doctoral studies, funded by the Social Sciences and Humanities Research Council of Canada, at the University of Victoria. He has published academic papers, essays, criticisms, fiction, and poetry in English, Persian, and German.

Dan Veach is coeditor and translator of *Flowers of Flame* (2008), the first anthology of poetry by Iraqis since the beginning of the Iraq war. His book of Chinese translations, *Wang River Poems*, is forthcoming.

Stephen Watts was born in London, England, in 1952. He has published three books of poetry and edited several anthologies. He has translated some works of contemporary Kurdish, Slovenian, and Persian poets, and has compiled a bibliography of twentieth century poetry in English translation due to be published online.

William Wolak has translated works of Joyce Mansour, Stuart Merrill, and Francis Vielé-Griffin. His Hafez cotranslations in this anthology are from *Your Lover's Beloved: Fifty-One Ghazals by Hafez* (2009), which he cotranslated with Mahmood Karimi-Hakak. Wolak is a published poet and an adjunct professor in the English Department at William Paterson University.

Sholeh Wolpé is the author of *Rooftops of Tehran*, *The Scar Saloon*, and

*Sin: Selected Poems of Forugh Farrokhzad* for which she was awarded the Lois Roth Persian Translation Prize in 2010. Wolpé is the editor of this anthology, a regional editor of *Tablet & Pen: Literary Landscapes from the Modern Middle East* edited by Reza Aslan, and the guest editor of *Atlanta Review* (2010 Iran issue). Her poems, translations, essays, and reviews have appeared in scores of literary journals, periodicals, and anthologies worldwide, and have been translated into several languages.

RASOUL YOUNAN was born in 1961 in Iran. He is the author of several collections of poetry, a novel, and a play.

NIMA YUSHIJ was born in 1897 in the village of Yush in Mazandaran, Iran. He wrote most of his books based on sorrow and suffering. Although this style was criticized by many, he believed that reflecting on deep-rooted problems will help to deal with them better. His influence on the evolution of modern poetry in Iran should not be underestimated. He became known to many as the father of modern Persian poetry in the years that followed. He died in 1959.

MANDANA ZANDIAN was born in March 1972 in Isfahan, Iran. She is the author of four volumes of poetry. After graduating from medical school in 2000, she moved to Los Angeles where she currently lives with her family.